201 Unique Ways to
MAKE YOUR
WEDDING SPECIAL

201 Unique Ways to
MAKE YOUR
WEDDING SPECIAL

Don Altman

MOON LAKE MEDIA
LOS ANGELES, CA

Fourth Printing 1997

While the author and publisher have done everything possible to find interesting ideas and concepts, we assume no responsibility or liability for inaccuracies, errors, omissions, inconsistencies, or products and services rendered in the creation of any and all of the ideas in this book. Any slights of people or organizations are fully unintentional. When deciding how to conduct all aspects of their weddings, readers must use their own best judgment and should consult with wedding coordinators or consultants if necessary.

Library of Congress Cataloging-in-Publication Data

Altman, Don, 1950-
    201 unique ways to make your wedding special /
      Don Altman.
      p. cm.
    Enl. ed. of: 151 unique ways to make your wedding special. c1994
    Includes index.
    ISBN 0-9639161-4-9 (alk. paper)
    1. Wedding etiquette. 2. Marriage customs and rites--United States. I. Altman, Don, 1950- 151 unique ways to make your wedding special. II. Title.
BJ2051.A48 1997
395.2'2--dc21
                                 97-15175
                                   CIP

Printed in the United States of America

ACKNOWLEDGMENTS:

I wish to thank those who supported my efforts to complete this book. Their feedback and sharing of ideas will always be appreciated: Tara Rashid; Mike and Phebe Arlen of Arlen Advertising; John Morley; Michele Rifkin; Sanda Sein, for creative input and for always being there; Jason Young, illustrator; Old Eyes, Weese, Otis, Dinz and "The Boys"; Mom, Dad, Jim, Debbie, Cindy and Paul—thanks for everything.

This book is dedicated to those couples beginning a new life together. May you create an event memorable enough to last you a lifetime!

PREFACE:

Why a book about unique wedding ideas? The answer may be found by thinking for a moment about those weddings you most remember. Does something special about them jog your memory? Probably. Then there's another reason: Terrific, creative ideas are hard to find. Searching for great wedding ideas is a lot like choosing art for your home. The selection process takes forever, but when you find something that works, voila! You know it instantly.

The idea for this book came into being while spending several months researching for a project that I created with my good friends, video producers Ridgie and Buttons Barton. The result was a comprehensive "how-to" video called *The Dream Wedding: Down-To-Earth Budget Video*. During the making of that video I discovered a shortage of wedding concepts that were truly creative, romantic and special. Before long, I found myself seeking out the best wedding ideas.

Bear in mind that no idea is 100% original. Even all of Shakespeare's plays are derivative. What's most important, however, is that he imprinted them all with his own inimitable style. That's a good way to view these wedding ideas. Take them just as they are, or use them to jump start your own creative energies. Either way, you'll inevitably end up making them your own.

There is probably no one event that better epitomizes the dreams of two people than a wedding. It expresses the way in which bride and groom relate to others and how they want others to relate to them. Because it's so personal, it's no wonder that everyone who gets married wants their wedding day to be truly special and memorable. The purpose of this book is to help make that dream become a reality.

FOREWORD:

As a professional, experienced wedding consultant and coordinator, I have witnessed a gradual evolution in wedding styles. In years past, wedding guidelines and styles were often dictated by rules of etiquette. Today, things have changed, and those "rules" are usually made to fit a couple's preferences and need for expression.

"New freedom" weddings of the '90s are more fun and memorable, and allow couples to express their love and elation through unique wedding locations, attire, culinary choices and all the other elements of a modern day wedding affair. However, this "new freedom" of expression is not entirely free of problems; achieving the outcome you demand ties in with having a competent facilitator to help you evaluate creative ideas and styles for this most special day of your life!

Fortunately, there's a handy resource and reference guide designed for couples and professionals in need of bright, new ideas: *201 Unique Ways to Make Your Wedding Special*. I've found the book to be a treasure-trove of creative concepts covering most every wedding category.

The information is well organized, and delivered with imagination and flair by the author—Don Altman—a documentary and Emmy Award winning writer who researched and compiled an "all-in-one-collection" to assist you in fulfilling your once-in-a-lifetime dream wedding.

Hosting a bland affair which doesn't portray the bride and groom's personal feelings is to miss out on a grand opportunity. Whether you are a do-it-yourselfer or an expert consultant, the goal is the same: Prevent wedding boredom!

If your wedding is worth making, then it's worth making special with *201 Unique Ways to Make Your Wedding Special*!

> —Sue-nett
> *Owner of "For Your Assistance," a wedding consulting and coordinating firm located in Thousand Oaks, California.*

TABLE OF CONTENTS:

Introduction: Who Can Use This Book?

Introduction

WHO CAN
USE THIS BOOK?

The answer is simple: Virtually anyone who wants to avoid wedding boredom and create a once-in-a-lifetime event! A wedding is a complex exercise in planning and organization. Because it consists of so many varied elements, a successful wedding must coordinate its many parts into a cohesive whole. When done right, the result is as seamless as a well directed movie.

For self-planners, this book will ensure that you don't forget to see the forest for the trees! Coordination and planning are one thing; shaping and designing a wedding that reflects your unique tastes, sensibilities and dreams is quite another. The ideas presented here will arm you with a host of brand new ideas. Most importantly, since you don't plan weddings every day, you'll have a lot of great options to choose from.

What about those people who hire professional wedding consultants or coordinators? Or for that matter, wedding consultants themselves? This book is for you, too. While experienced planners have a storehouse of contacts and concepts, good consultants also enjoy discovering new ideas. The sharing of ideas between consultants and clients opens up a dialogue and gets the creative juices flowing. Ideally, it should bring out issues of style and help focus in on what the bride and groom want. It's an important step in making any dream wedding come true.

As an added practical benefit, the Appendix consists of a Wedding Resource Guide which includes a valuable list of mail order catalogs, products and services. So wherever the bride and groom live, they can get a head start in locating and obtaining many of the ideas mentioned here. This useful tool also includes nationwide, computerized bridal registries with toll-free numbers.

1

For ease of use, chapter headings are alphabetical and arranged by topic. Simply scan the Table of Contents to find the right subject. I hope the information contained here informs, entertains and helps make your wedding journey a fascinating and fruitful one.

CHAPTER 1

BACHELOR PARTIES
FOR REAL MEN

Bachelor parties are more interesting, fun and creative than ever before. In other words, there's a lot less drinking and leering. Here are eighteen fun alternatives to the traditional bachelor party of years past.

Beach Party

Grab the volleyball, the Frisbee, lots of snack food, an ice chest, the suntan lotion and a pair of comfortable sandals. Then head down to the nearest beach. To make this bachelor party a success, simply play all day and watch the sun go down over the water. If desired, invite the bride-to-be and her friends over for an evening lobster bake and a beach party that even the *Baywatch* crowd would envy.

Camping Party

With the help of the bride or one of the guys, plan to kidnap the bachelor. Make sure to have a camera on hand so the event can be captured for posterity. Caravan to the site, and hunker down for the weekend if time allows.

There's nothing like camping out as a male bonding experience. After two days of roughing it with the guys, the bachelor will be more than glad to get back home!

Concert/Event Party

For bachelors who appreciate live concerts, this could be

an experience to remember. Remember, concerts needn't be limited to music. This bachelor party could take place at a jazz club, a playhouse, a piano bar or a hip comedy club. If it's a comedy club, sit up front for maximum exposure.

Crafts Party

Who says that guys aren't creative? Give the bachelor and his friends a chance to express themselves by finding either a ceramics or woodworking teacher willing to give a group class. If ceramics is chosen, the group can make gifts for the bridesmaids, as well as present a prize for the best—and worst—ceramics.

After sculpting and shaping clay for an afternoon, the bachelor artists will have earned a hearty meal. If wood making or refinishing is the manly activity of choice, then have the group refinish a piece of antique furniture to be presented to the bachelor as a gift.

Cruise Ship Party

Depending on the bachelor's home town, there are cruise lines that offer two- or three-day cruises. One cruise line in California, for example, travels from Los Angeles to Catalina Island to Ensenada, Mexico and back. There are also riverboat cruises that traverse the Mississippi. (see Appendix, Page 119)

Dude Ranch Party

Just like in the movie, *City Slickers*, take a bachelor on a "last roundup." Most dude ranches have cabins large enough to sleep six or eight. In the morning, the group can go for a ride on horseback, only to stop for a trail feast of flapjacks, bacon and eggs cooked fresh over the campfire.

Some dude ranches feature wagon rides, square dancing and swimming pools. It's a super way to combine the out-of-doors with down home comfort.

Fishing/Yachting Party

Hemingway would have endorsed this style of bachelor party. One-day fishing excursions out on the lake or the deep blue sea can take a bachelor group in search of that elusive "big one." Or rent a yacht that has all the pleasures of home.

Gambling Party

Strictly legal, of course, hold this party at a racetrack or even a big-time venue like Las Vegas or Atlantic City. Take in an evening show, sample excellent food, and play for big stakes. Or steaks, if that's a bachelor's pleasure. If the excursion is to the racetrack, try renting a private box for the whole group.

Golfing Party

This party requires bachelors who are avid golfers and want to spend a day out on the links. The game could be played in such a way that the bachelor gets a prize for each hole he wins. The good thing about golf is that the festivities can naturally continue at the 19th hole—in the clubhouse and the restaurant.

Pool Party

Rent out a local pool, or use a pool at a condo or someone's house. Then bring in some pizza, or barbecue if there is a chef among the group. Don't forget a ball for a spirited game of water polo.

River Rafting Party

There are rafting trips for every taste and expense. These can range from weekend trips down local rapids in small rubber rafts to week long excursions through the Grand Canyon in giant pontoon boats that culminate in a hair-raising ride down the renowned Lava Falls.

Roasting Party

If the bachelor has long-time friends, then there are probably enough stories with which to "roast" him in good fun. Try to find a surprise guest, or locate embarrassing pictures from that ancient high school yearbook.

Skiing Party

For bachelors who love to ski, there's nothing more invigorating than a weekend at a ski resort. Beginners in the group can get lessons, and when evening rolls around, bachelors can share stories of the day's adventures while soaking in the Jacuzzi.

Sports Party

If the bachelor is into sports, there are numerous choices available. Have a baseball party for spring, summer or fall events. Some stadiums have clubhouse rooms that can be rented. That way the group will have its own space while rooting for its favorite team. Go to a night game, and the party can continue afterwards. A football party is great for both fall and winter seasons.

If the bachelor doesn't want to go to the game, consider a sports bar and watch the game on a big screen TV.

Theme Park Party

Take the bachelor and his friends for an afternoon trip to an amusement park or theme park. Many of the rides are strictly for the bold and brave. Plus, bachelors can test their macho quotient by trying to ring the bell with the sledge hammer and by playing for prizes at the park's many challenging arcade games. Then, if all stomachs are in reasonable shape, make a trip out to dinner to top off the evening.

Volleyball Party

For bachelors near the beach, volleyball and surf go together like "surf and turf." As the sun goes down, finish things off with a tasty lobster or clam bake.

Waterpark Party

Here's a great way to experience the thrill of river rafting without packing up the gear and leaving town. The group will enjoy an exhilarating day in the sun while sliding down water chutes. After building up an appetite, plan on having lunch at a favorite restaurant or enjoy a barbecue in the backyard.

Wine and Cheese Tasting Party

This party is ideal for the bachelor who appreciates fine wines. Try putting together a selection of wines from the bachelor's favorite vintner, including a special wine that he can share with his bride-to-be. For non-drinkers, be sure to include sparkling cider and juice. Of course, where there's wine there's cheese. Include a variety of mouth-watering soft and hard cheeses with crackers and French bread.

To make the party complete, surprise the bachelor with some keepsake gifts. A number of wine-related products—ranging from apparel to private label wines—are available. (see Appendix, Pages 121-123)

CHAPTER 2

BEVERAGES
WET, WILD AND WILLING

Open, fully-stocked bars are still part of the wedding repertoire. But with fewer people drinking hard liquor, interesting alternatives are appreciated. More often than not these non-alcoholic "brews" are easy on the budget.

Fruit Punch Fountain with Ice Sculpture

What's that colorful liquid gushing from the fountain? It must be a zesty fruit punch. To enhance the fruit punch fountain's ambiance, place it in front of an ice sculpture. These sculptures can be made in almost any size you desire. Caterers can arrange for fountains and ice sculptures. Some food wholesalers may sell ice sculpture molds if the bride and groom are interested in making their own. As a final touch, sprinkle pesticide-free flower petals in the fountain.

Premium Water and Juice Bar

Those who like to go *au naturel* have a wide variety of elegant glacier, spring and sparkling waters to choose from. For the purest water on earth, choose glacier water. (It has the fewest parts per million of dissolved solids of any water.) Natural spring waters have that inviting, crisp taste. And sparkling mineral waters come in combination flavors, from cherry and strawberry to lemon-kiwi and orange-mango.

Natural juices and iced teas nicely supplement waters. The number of products to choose from is mind-numbing, from a 100% pure juice concoction like pineapple-orange-banana to a cranberry-cherry mineral juice drink. So go to a health store, organic food mart or even the local grocery chain store to find a swimmingly good selection.

Private Label Wine and Champagne

Have the bride and groom ever fantasized about having their own winery? Now is the perfect opportunity! Many restaurants and hotels have private label brands of premium waters and juices; couples can also order a private label wine or champagne for their special day. Several companies will place a label of your choice onto one of their products. The message on the label can say "Especially bottled for..." with the names of the bride and groom and wedding date. (see Appendix, Pages 121-122)

Viennese Coffee Bar

Coffees have become one of the most popular drinks around. There's an extensive variety of styles, such as espresso, café latte, cappuccino and everything in between. Add almond or vanilla flavoring for a tantalizing treat. Spice up the drinks further by adding brandy, amaretto and other liqueurs. Besides, there's nothing like that big, impressive cappuccino machine to stimulate the taste buds.

Imagine how much fun guests will have over at the "Viennese coffee bar" or "international coffee bar." While many restaurants and hotels offer this kind of alcoholic substitute, a coffee bar can also be acquired through off-site caterers. And, though it is usually open prior to the reception, the coffee bar can also be open when cake and dessert are served.

White Bar

Instead of providing hard liquor, there's a lighter choice. It's known as a "white bar" and includes drinks such as champagne and wine. These lighter alternatives are both classy and perfect for brunch or afternoon affairs when drinking isn't as prevalent.

If desired, the white bar can be expanded by adding some basic alcoholic drinks, such as a clear rum, gin and vodka. If economy is important, offer less expensive "well brands" rather than name-brand, premium liquors.

CHAPTER 3

BOUQUETS FOR THE SWEET SCENT OF ROMANCE

Leaf through any bridal magazine, and most show a bride holding a colorful floral bouquet. Bridesmaids' bouquets are typically similar, but understated. Here's an opportunity to do something creative and different.

Bridal Bouquet Keepsake

Here are a few ideas for the bride who wants to preserve her bridal bouquet. Of course, this means getting a second, less elaborate bouquet which the bride can toss, while keeping the real one for herself.

Bridal bouquets can be saved in a number of different artistic arrangements: Preserve them in their original wedding bouquet shape, under a glass dome or as pressed flowers suitable for shadow box framing. Keep in mind, however, that not all flowers can be dried and preserved. Find out in advance what kinds of flowers are best to include in a bouquet. After the wedding, the bouquet flowers can be separated and dried, then reassembled.

Craft, hobby and art stores are an excellent place to locate books like *Flower Drying Art with Silicon Gel* and *The Best Drying Flower Book*, which can teach the bride how to dry her own flowers. A book called *Magical Microwave Flower Drying* teaches all about the new microwave flower drying technique. Generally, certain flowers can be air dried while others require silicon gel. Either way, the flowers should be prepared for drying as soon as possible.

Flowers best for drying include the anemone, aster, baby's breath, bachelor button, button mum, carnation, camellia, dahlia, dogwood, larkspur, lilac, magnolia, marigold, pansy, poppy, rose, snap dragon, statice and violet to name a few.

Which flowers should be avoided? The difficult-to-preserve list includes tulips and other bulb flowers, as well as tropical flowers that are typically succulent. Steer clear of iris, orchids and gardenias.

Even after drying, some flowers may still be vulnerable to humidity, which can alter the color or cause crumbling. Since the bride is putting so much effort into maintaining her bouquet, it might be worth applying a finish sealer to protect this keepsake. Then, place the flowers back in their holder or make a new arrangement to cherish and enjoy.

If flower preservation is too much to worry about while packing for the honeymoon, there's the option of finding a company that will preserve flowers after the wedding. For example, one company provides a special temperature-controlled shipping box which is returned to them after the wedding. The flowers are then arranged in a three-dimensional, shadow box display. (see Appendix, Page 123)

Bridesmaids' Baskets

If flowers are the choice for bridesmaids, why not use them creatively with the addition of a miniature basket? Fill the small basket to overflowing with an arrangement of bright springtime flowers. Carnations, daisies, mums, pansies and forget-me-nots create a country fresh feeling ideal for backyard or garden weddings.

Since bridesmaids' bouquets allow for a certain amount of creativity and latitude, consider attaching a dainty flower arrangement onto a neck band or a hat. Or the bride could do as Lauren Bacall did when she married Humphrey Bogart: Pin a modest bouquet onto the dress itself. (see Appendix, Pages 112; 121)

Bridesmaids' Dried Flower Bouquet

Dried bouquets are an excellent fresh flower substitute. Plus, there's no having to worry about drying them *after* the wedding. Dried flowers can be quite beautiful, consisting of delicate, dried roses and baby's breath or any favorite dried flowers. And, like bridesmaids' fans, dried flower bouquets make an ideal keepsake.

Bridesmaids' Fans

Throughout history, fans have been a popular item in many cultures. Ornately decorated fans, from Victorian to modern, create a special flair for bridesmaids. When a standard ten inch fan is opened up to a span of sixteen inches across, the result is dramatic.

Check out antique stores and shows to find such authentic Victorian fans. Folding lace fans are nicely suited to outdoor or Southern weddings. These fans can be embellished with silk or fresh flowers and bows. For a different look, the whole fan, including embellishments, can be stiffened to a porcelain finish using craft store products.

Custom fans can be constructed out of various materials to achieve unusual results. For example, custom designs can be painted on large sheets of rice paper. The result after pleating is a soft, yet modern fan. Another material to consider is fabric. Most any fabric will do, although you'll need to use liquid starch or another stiffener so the fan will hold its shape.

Brides might want to tell bridesmaids that back in the old days, fans were used for flirting. The speed with which a woman fanned and the way in which they opened and closed their fan sent a particular message...so be careful!

Bridesmaids' Western Style Bouquet

For a western wedding, here's a beautiful and unique western bridal bouquet that lends a Native American slant. Start by rounding up strands or streamers of turquoise and pearl beads. These can hang from a white and aqua satin flower center. Add a few leaves, made of satin or silk, to the flowers. For the quintessential western touch, add some puffy white feathers to the turquoise and pearl strands.

CHAPTER 4

BRIDAL ATTIRE
(see WEDDING ATTIRE)

BRIDAL SHOWERS
THAT KEEP ON GIVING

Since there were eighteen bachelor parties in Chapter 1, in the interest of fairness here are an equal number of ways to amuse, entertain and shower a bride-to-be with gifts. None of the following will take the place of lingerie, bath and general showers, but they can add spice and a personalized touch to smaller, intimate gatherings.

Angel Shower

The angel craze continues, and with it come angels for almost any occasion, especially bridal showers. There are angels on mirrors, candles, wind chimes, picture frames, candle holders, pillows, paper weights, decorative plates, mugs, notebooks, pendants and music CDs, to name just a few. Any bride who loves angels will long remember this gathering of her own personal angels.

Book, CD and Video Shower

This is perfect for the bride who likes to read, listen to music or watch movies. There are many accessories to books, CDs and videos that make fine gifts. For example, there are page holders, book ends, CD shelves and video tape rewinding machines. If the guests really know the bride's tastes, they can find some very personalized gifts. (see Appendix, Pages 114-115; 123)

Baking Shower

Stir things up by introducing would-be baker-brides to a mix of interesting products. Rolling pins, measuring cups and spoons, paring knives, spatulas, cookie cutters, gingerbread molds, pie shells, pastry blender and brush, frosting decoration tools, and even some flour and ingredients will get them started. Don't forget a bakery cookbook. As an added incentive, have the ingredients to bake an apple pie on hand and then serve it hot, a la mode. (see Appendix, Pages 115-117)

Collectibles Shower

You can't get much more personalized than this. But it only works if the bride or couple has a collection of something—such as plates, antique cups or mugs. A collectibles shower is ideal for a more intimate group.

Gadget and Game Shower

By combining bar ware and breakfast gadgets with games, this shower offers both variety and entertainment. For bar ware gadgets, there are many items to choose from, such as goblets, corkscrews, swizzle sticks, coasters, tumblers and blenders. Breakfast gadget gifts include non-stick pans, breakfast-in-bed trays, toasters, egg cups and trivets.

After looking at the gadgets, it's time for the games to begin. This is especially good for couples who love to gather with friends to play *Monopoly* and other such games. There are hundreds of entertaining card games, strategy games and physical games available. The nice thing about this portion of the shower is that participants can select one of the games and try it out on the spot.

Green Thumb Shower

There's nothing that helps to make a house feel like home more than plants. Big plants and small plants, from cactus and herbs to ferns and bonsai, and all in between, will beautify and enliven this shower. Don't forget vases and watering cans. Even small fruit trees, such as apple and orange trees, can be planted in the backyard and enjoyed for years. Have each plant-giver write instructions on a little card that tell how to care for the plant. (see Appendix, Page 115)

Home Office Shower

If the bride and groom are among the growing cadre of those who work out of the home, then they'll appreciate the variety of items found here. Included are practical items such as a pen and pencil set, stationery holder, computerized accounting program, wall picture, clock, coffee mug, fax machine, calendar, daily organizer, telephone answering machine, dictionary and desk lamp. (see Appendix, Page 121)

Hot 'N Spicy Shower

There are plenty of hot and spicy themed items—from food and spices to clothing and music—to satisfy any taste for the exotic. Each guest can bring a "hot and spicy" gift from a different category. Or, stick with food if that's a particular passion of the bride and groom.

For those with a hankering for spicy foods, there are decorative and edible wreaths and garlands made of red hot chile peppers, garlic bulbs, basil, oregano, bay leaves and sun dried tomatoes. Pour on the heat with a variety of salsas, chimichuri sauces, chipotle seasonings and chile dips. (see Appendix, Page 116)

There's kitchenware galore to accompany these fixings. And make sure someone brings salsa and blue corn chips as a shower snack.

Jewelry Shower

If the bride likes to wear costume jewelry, this could be a natural. And as a finishing touch, the hostess of the shower could give her a jewelry box to put it all in.

Keepsake Shower

After the wedding, the bride will have accumulated several keepsakes. This shower will bring together those essential elements, such as the garter, a memory book, toasting flutes, ring-bearer pillows, pen sets for the guest book, an engraved purse mirror and more.

The one "must" item to include at this shower?—a personalized, wedding keepsake box for organizing and storing all those great memories. When adorned with the right decorations, an ordinary hat box can be transformed into a one-of-a-kind keepsake box.

Month of the Year Shower

The only rule for this shower is that each participant bring a gift relating to a different month or season of the year. Since each month relates to a particular flower, color and gemstone, gifts containing these should be easy to find. And, don't forget about those seasonal items that come in handy, too.

Perfume Shower

This shower could include not just perfume, but most any sweet-smelling substance—like potpourri, incense, aroma therapy oils, room fresheners and scented candles.

Recipe Shower

Each person coming to the shower is instructed to bring a favorite recipe card, along with an item that goes along with that recipe. For instance, an angel food cake recipe might also come with an angel food cake pan. All the recipes are placed into a handy card file as a keepsake and the bride goes home with recipes and cookware for preparing all kinds of goodies.

Tea and Coffee Shower

If coffee or tea is the bride's bag, then this shower is the brew for her. She will be able to start every day with items like gourmet coffee, large cappuccino mugs, coffee makers, grinders and other accessories.

Tea lovers will appreciate everything from basic English Tea to non-caffeinated herbal tea to exotic, aromatic loose teas such as mango. There are many gourmet honeys to choose from, too. For tea accessories galore, consider fine china cups and saucers, tea pots and strainers, tea towels, spoons and ice tea makers. Excellent aroma therapy teas and health teas like *Golden Seal Herb* are available in most health stores. (see Appendix, Pages 115-117)

Time of the Day Shower

This shower produces an interesting and eclectic array of gift items because each guest brings items typically used during a specific time of the day. One guest may be assigned 7-9 a.m., another 12-2 p.m., yet another 9-11 p.m., and so on. This shower is ideal for coed gatherings because there's enough latitude to find things that work equally well for both bride and groom.

Time Capsule Shower

Every single moment in time is unique. With a time capsule shower, the bride-to-be gets to cherish and save her special bridal moments for posterity. The idea is for all the participants to bring memorabilia to "store" in a time capsule that will be opened at a future date in time—such as a 25th wedding anniversary or other significant event. The time capsule itself consists of a decorated, sealable container that the hostess or group has prepared for the shower. If desired, the time capsule can be decorated and sealed right at the party.

What kinds of items or keepsakes can be stored in the time capsule? Include photos of the bride-to-be's new house or apartment, headlines, a popular music CD, a video and other personal mementos. Remember to include letters to the future written by everyone who is present—including the bride and groom. When unsealed, the time capsule shower will provide wonderful memories and even possibly, a few nostalgic collectibles to pass on to the next generation! (see Appendix, Page 119)

Wedding Quilt Shower

The idea is to have all the guests participate in the making of a beautiful quilt for the couple to keep. Not only is the quilt a personalized keepsake, but it's practical and beautiful as well.

Here's how the shower works: A seamstress/hostess sends out an 8" to 10" square of white or colored cotton material to all the participants. Everyone is instructed to draw a picture or message on the material. The picture must represent something of importance to the couple and should also be signed. Don't worry—the needed cross-stitch doesn't require an expert. When finished, the squares are sent back to the hostess, who performs her magic. The completed work is a big, colorful, fluffy wedding quilt guaranteed to make for one of the bride's most beloved shower gifts.

Wine Lover's Shower

If the bride and groom are wine enthusiasts, surprise them with a wealth of wine-related items. Even the novice wine aficionado will appreciate the kinds of products that are available, including vacuum seals that keep wine fresh after opening, bottle tags for organizing a wine collection, wine racks and cellars of every size and sophistication, wreaths made of wine corks, antique-style wine openers, guide books for wine buyers and wine glasses for every occasion. For that extra special, customized shower gift, consider a personalized plaque to be placed in the wine cellar. (see Appendix, Page 123)

CHAPTER 5

CAKES QUIXOTIC, TRENDY AND TASTY

Wedding cakes attract attention like a powerful magnet. Cakes can be tremendously creative and original. So ask bakers for pictures of cakes they've made, and begin to map out a just dessert.

Airbrushed Cakes

Airbrushing is a method of painting that creates a particular look similar to that smooth, sweeping style found on the side of custom vans. Believe it or not, airbrush artists can actually paint pictures on the frosting of the cake. How do they do it? With food coloring, of course.

Using airbrush technique, wedding cakes can be decorated with some dramatic and novel results. How about a portrait of the bride and groom? A mutual love or passion? Or a scene depicting the place where the couple first met?

Bridesmaids' Charms

One interesting custom that involves bridesmaids is cake ribbon pulling. Small sterling silver or gold plated charms are placed beneath the cake's frosting. Naturally, the charms are put in place *before* the frosting is applied. Each charm is attached to a ribbon, which a bridesmaid pulls out prior to the cake cutting.

There are many fascinating and wonderful charms to choose from, and legend has it that the bridesmaid who chooses the token ring charm is next in line to be married.

Cake Decorations

If there's something really custom the bride and groom desire, but it can't be located as a cake topper, don't despair. With filigree icing, bakers can design almost anything, be it edible ribbons, tennis rackets or horse heads. If family tradition is meaningful, think about using family crests or letters to adorn the cake top or sides.

The magic of frosting can help attain an array of effects, including lace, ribbons, pearls and tulle. Using a mixture of sugar and shortening known as rolled fondant will help create an ultra smooth texture.

Don't forget the beauty of fresh flowers. No matter how often we see them, flower-decorated cakes always seem unique. Best of all, the sprinkling of fresh flower petals helps to make even a simple cake look more tasteful and elegant. In fact, letters can be spelled out using flower petals. Just be sure the petals are fresh and have not been exposed to pesticides.

Here's a final word about how to achieve flower power: As an alternative to fresh flowers, consider using sugar flowers to match the color scheme. (see Appendix, Page 112)

Cakes with Design in Mind

Sometimes, the bride and groom want a cake to represent something for which they have a passion. There's no reason this can't be done, within reason and within budget! For example, an architect might want a cake to represent his/her favorite design period—from neoclassical to modern. A fashion designer might want a cake to resemble a quilt or other fabric. For avid publishers, writers or readers, the cake could resemble a favorite volume of books. A cake can even represent a fairy tale castle or a favorite locale, such as the Leaning Tower of Pisa and the Great Pyramids.

Will cake makers take on your dream cake? Probably, since most like the opportunity to try something different. Gold domes and columns are not all that difficult. In fact, neither are heart-shaped designs.

Wedding and culinary magazines are rich sources for locating cake ideas. Look in the phone book to find local bakers and cake designers. When visiting them, make sure to look at pictures of cakes they've designed. One word of caution, however. Multi-tiered cakes need a filling that can support all those layers. So take care to avoid soft fillings such as those made of mousse.

Gazebo Cake

Many wedding cakes feature small gazebos on the top layer. But how about a whole cake designed as a gazebo? The top covering of the gazebo could be decorated in a layer of flower petals, or feature a particular design. For a realistic look, the gazebo cake can be airbrushed throughout—and even including portraits of the bride and groom. Get pictures of gazebos for the cake designer to work from, and consider making the wickerwork out of white chocolate. The nice thing about this cake is that the bride and groom can have their gazebo and eat it too!

Music Box Cake Topper and More

There are music box cake toppers that play *The Wedding March*, as well as many other tunes. One company, *The San Francisco Music Box Company* (see Appendix, Page 122), offers a variety of delightful and romantic wedding cake toppers that play music to boot.

For unusual cake toppers, peruse the local model shop, or look in magazines and discover miniatures of almost anything to put atop or beside the cake—from scale model Corvettes and his and hers Harley-Davidsons, to tiny plastic baseball caps championing the couple's favorite team.

Photographic Cake

Imagine high resolution, near-photographic color photos of the bride and groom painted on a wedding cake. It's now possible, thanks to computer equipment that scans the photo and a device that sprays food dye onto a cake's white frosted surface. Any picture will do, as long as the top of the cake has a smooth and flat surface.

Tiramisu Cake

Tiramisu is the delectable, rich and creamy dessert found on dessert trays at Italian restaurants. This tasty confection can also be used as a cake filling that will be a treat to all, including the non-Italian guests.

Victorian Fan Cake

A cake that is designed to resemble an intricately laced Victorian fan is ideal for those couples having a Victorian themed wedding. This is appropriate, since no one symbol better represents the traditional Victorian courtship than the well-recognized Victorian fan. Provide the cake designer or baker with designs based on real Victorian fans. Choose elements from one or more fans to incorporate into the cake.

Wedgwood Cake

Wedgwood, a venerable name synonymous with being the best in porcelain work and refined design can be replicated on a cake. A Wedgwood cake might complement a wedding with an English high tea, especially if the tea cups and platters are the one and only Wedgwood.

CHAPTER 6

CATERING WITH UNUSUALLY GOOD TASTE

With weddings being held at all times of the day and night, the traditional sit-down dinner has evolved into a number of mouth-watering variations.

The All-New Dessert Reception

This is a concept that is catching on. Dessert receptions are popular for the cost-conscious who want to be married in style. They're also popular for people marrying for the second time who don't want the complete sit-down dinner.

Typically, this kind of reception works in one of two ways: One is to have an intimate dinner for close family members, followed by a dessert reception for all the guests. A second style of dessert reception is to simply have an evening dessert reception which immediately follows the ceremony. Be sure to note "dessert reception to follow" on the invitations. That way guests will know to eat dinner in advance.

Sweet tables can incorporate just about any delectable indulgence imaginable, including a variety of mousses, cheesecakes, turnovers, puffs, fresh fruit tarts, cakes, custard-filled pastries, petit fours, chocolate German cakes, cheeses and chocolate-dipped fruit. Strawberry tuxedoes (extra large strawberries dipped in dark and white chocolate to resemble tuxedoes) are one popular dipped fruit.

Since dessert receptions begin later in the evening, a full bar might not be necessary. In that case, consider offering a Viennese coffee bar. (see Chapter 2, Beverages)

Angel Ice Cubes

Here's an opportunity to add a unique finishing touch to catering efforts. Guests won't help but notice that the ice cubes floating in the punch are molded in the shape of delicate little angels, flowers, hearts, or other meaningful shapes. These molds can be found at art and kitchenware stores. If desired, the ice cubes can easily be colored.

English High Tea

Tired of the same old fish, poultry, or meat choices on wedding menus? Then think about having a *high tea* for your wedding. A *what*, you ask?

Here's the scoop on the high tea: It's an Old World custom dating back to England in the 1800s. It's gaining popularity today because it lends late morning or afternoon weddings a look that is distinctive, elegant, and creative, while still keeping all the traditional values and historical meaning of the wedding ceremony.

Traditionally, a high tea contains a combination of *savories* and *sweets*. The savories, consisting of such things as sandwiches and appetizers, are the equivalent of a first course. One traditional high tea sandwich is the English cucumber and tomato sandwich on brown bread with butter. There's also a delectable variety of puffs and pastry cups filled with chicken salad and garnished with fresh herbs and squash. Include a less traditional, but a very rich, Stilton and walnut tort served with herb toast and fresh vegetables. High teas also include a variety of fresh cheeses to spread on vegetables. To make the tea memorable and special, some even offer unusual items such as quail eggs.

Sweets at a high tea can be presented with the cake cutting, or with the savories. One very traditional sweet is English chocolate chip pound cake served with fresh strawberries. Then as a garnish, add some mushrooms dipped in caramel and chocolate. For another tasty tea dessert, try light-as-air, custard-filled puffs drizzled in chocolate. Standard fare at any high tea are scrumptious scones with currants. Scones are sweet biscuits that are usually served with clotted cream or Devonshire cream, plus a variety of jams and fruit butters. Sound rich? You bet! In England they split the scones in half and spread on the goodies.

Beverages served at a high tea include the traditional Earl Grey or other hot tea, as well as coffee, if desired. In addition, a sherry is usually served with both savories and sweets.

For those people unfamiliar with a high tea, the quantity of food served is substantial enough to feed the hungriest of guests. Plus it provides a variety of foods not usually found at a typical wedding meal.

The high tea allows for additional site flexibility since most of the items are prepared in advance and do not require a full kitchen. High teas require fewer servers, so this may be an added bonus to the budget. While some caterers provide beautiful linen, silver and china as part of their service, others charge for renting these items. So always find out what's included.

In short, if the bride and groom are looking for a unique catering option that's lavish, yet typically not as expensive as a sit-down meal, then consider the high tea.

Sushi Bar Hors D'oeuvres Station

Guests will flock to this station just to watch the sushi chef prepare these exotic hors d'oeuvres. Some hotels have sushi restaurants, which makes obtaining a sushi bar easier. But even if there's no sushi bar at the wedding site, there are sushi restaurants that will gladly set up an off-site sushi bar.

Wok Hors D'oeuvres Station

Tired of over-crispy, microwaved hors d'oeuvres? Then consider having freshly cooked hors d'oeuvres. A wok station can do just that. The wok chef will stir up all kinds of magic in the wok pan. Guests will relish all the fresh veggies, shrimp and seafood, teriyaki chicken and other delicacies made to order. In keeping with the Oriental food theme, offer Chinese chicken salad, egg rolls and spicy Szechwan pot stickers.

CHAPTER 7

CENTERPIECES GUARANTEED TO CAPTIVATE

Typically, centerpieces consist of fresh flowers. But more and more people are choosing centerpieces limited only by the imagination.

Birdcage Centerpiece

This decorative birdcage is not intended to hold real birds. Found at many arts and crafts stores, these decorative cages may have frames of wicker or metal. Paint the frame white or the desired color, then drape it with an arrangement of flowers and ribbons. Then, complete this dramatic and compelling centerpiece by placing a sachet with potpourri, fruit or candle on the inside. (see Appendix, Pages 112; 121)

Bountiful Basket Centerpiece

Baskets of many sizes and shapes can be dressed up to match the wedding theme or decor. Baskets can be decorated in papier-mâché, painted and covered in fresh flowers. These individual art pieces can be filled with anything from flowers, candies, fruit, veggies and hors d'oeuvres and are sure to be coveted by guests as a take home gift.

Charity Centerpiece

Perhaps you're familiar with the phrase: "It is more blessed to give than to receive." Some couples take that to heart by building centerpiece sculptures made entirely of canned goods. Then, after the wedding, the cans are donated to the charity of choice. The variety of sizes and colors of labels make an impressive statement. A canned goods centerpiece can be attractive, too, if decorated with ribbons and bows that coordinate with the wedding colors. Also, arrange fresh flowers or dried flowers in between the cans.

There's no need to stick to canned goods. Make a centerpiece out of boxed foods, or anything else that the bride and groom's favorite charity might need. Imagination is the magic key!

Dessert Centerpiece

Edible centerpieces are a delectable dessert addition to the wedding cake. And of course, the variations are endless. One catering director recommends a chocolate swan centerpiece. The swan or another favorite design can be filled with fruit. Use a shape from the wedding theme. Or place fresh, seasonal fruit in the bowl.

Where does one locate these items? There are companies that make edible centerpieces out of white chocolate roses, chocolate swans, chocolate brides and grooms, chocolate champagne bottles and more. There are even wedding favors wrapped in color-coordinated ribbons which are made by the famous Belgian chocolatier company, Godiva. (see Appendix, 120) Caterers will also be able to locate these specialty items.

For custom, edible centerpieces, it's possible to locate and purchase molds from food wholesalers. Or, go to a bakery and see if they can help. The alternatives are endless, although one this author would personally like to see is a sculpture made out of chocolate chip cookies.

Flower Cookie Centerpiece

Here's a lip-smacking flower centerpiece made of edible flowers. The flower-shaped cookies are baked with a wooden skewer that serves as the flower's stem. After baking, the cookies can be covered with icing and trimming made of almost any color. All that's left is to pot the flower cookies in an attractive centerpiece vase or pot filled with florist's plastic foam. Fortunately, these edible flowers will never wilt—but they'll sure get nibbled.

Gardening Lover's Centerpiece

This centerpiece is ideal for gardening couples who also want to transfer a passion for gardening to others. Best of all, many of the ingredients can come from home gardens. Paint a galvanized gardening pail before filling it with a mix of flowers and vegetables, combining bright yellow sunflowers, daisies, and carnations with clusters of fresh cherry tomatoes, radishes, carrots and mint.

As a final touch, toss in some cheese, crusty bread and a packet of flower or vegetable seeds. This not only provides some fresh and tasty snacks, but who knows—it may inspire a whole new generation of gardeners!

Gingerbread House Centerpiece

Have you ever seen a real gingerbread house? Nibbling is practically irresistible. This enchanting centerpiece is a delicious snack to go along with the wedding cake. Instead of providing an individual gingerbread centerpiece for each table, have one large gingerbread house made for the head table. Letting the bride and groom break off the first pieces adds charm to the cake cutting ceremony.

Healthy Appetizer with Roses Centerpiece

Most people have experienced being at weddings and waiting for what seemed like hours before dinner arrived. That problem can be resolved by creating a vegetable platter centerpiece. Imagine a mountain of eggplants, zucchini, carrots, potatoes, jicama and radishes—all carved like roses. The healthy vegetable centerpiece would be garnished with delicate parsley, mint and other herbs. As a finishing touch, wrap the entire platter in a ribbon and bow. And, depending on the platter, some fresh flowers can be arranged around the veggies to create a true work of art.

A Pumpkin Centerpiece for Fall Seasons

For fall weddings, putting flowers in a pumpkin instead of a pot is just the beginning of a truly festive centerpiece. (No faces carved in the pumpkins, please.) If the color scheme is anything like tangerine and yellow, big fluffy fall flowers like daisies, carnations and mums will coordinate perfectly. Then add pussy willows and ferns to fill in the pumpkin vase. Around the pumpkin centerpiece place some red and yellow maple leaves, gourds, and colorful Indian or pueblo corn. To ensure that the pumpkin sits flat on the table, shave the bottom or level it with a knife.

For some variation, use smaller pumpkins at the guests' tables and a large pumpkin filled with fall flowers and foliage at the head table. And just think of all the pumpkin seeds to eat or give away as party favors to the guests!

Seashell Centerpiece

Ships ahoy! Sailors, sea lovers, collectors of seashells and romantics of all kinds delight in the many shapes and sizes of seashells. Large conch, clam and other shells can combine to form distinctive and dramatic centerpieces. And remember, this beautiful collection of shells can also be used to hold anything from mints and candies to fruit, veggies and hors d'oeuvres.

Topiary Centerpiece

Looking for a plant with great versatility? Topiary is thy name! More formal and larger than Japanese bonsai plants, topiaries were the rave in France around the time of King Louis XVI. Anyone who has seen a pruned hedge has seen a cousin of the topiary. Topiaries have small diameter trunks that rise about a foot high to green leafy tops.

Topiaries make stunning centerpieces. The tops can be trimmed heart-shaped, round, spherical, square or another geometric shape. They can even be trimmed to look like animals.

As dramatic as they are alone, topiaries can be dressed up dramatically. Flowering vines can be woven throughout, or fresh flowers of almost any variety can be placed in the mass of leaves. Depending on the look desired, dried flowers or silk flowers can also be arranged inside. For a touch of class, set topiaries in gold pots and wrap them in ribbons.

Topiaries are alive, so they can be taken home, watered and enjoyed for years to come. This is one centerpiece guests will fight over. Check with local florists and find out which ones have experience with topiaries. (see Appendix, Page 115)

Treasure Candle Centerpiece

Found in some gift shops, treasure or "wish" candles may contain coins, trinkets, rings, gems and other hidden goodies. When the candle melts, the prize inside the wax is revealed. These candles will be sought after as take-home gifts. And, their significance as a wedding centerpiece will long be remembered.

Enhance the treasure candle by surrounding it with a well-designed collection of bows, ribbons, flowers and greenery.

Wreath Centerpiece

Wreaths need not be seasonal symbols for Christmas or New Year's. A traditional Christmas style wreath—replete with holly, evergreen, red ribbon and mistletoe—makes for a great holiday wedding table decoration. But there are a variety of other wreaths to match most wedding tastes.

A dove, shaped out of white feathers, can take flight out of a wreath swathed in fern, ivy and gossamery white flowers. Spread spongy moss gently over the wreath's bottom, forming a pretty, natural bottom.

Wreaths come in various shapes and sizes. For a Valentine's Day wedding, obtain a heart-shaped wreath. Decorate it with simple, but elegant, dried roses and ribbons. Or embellish it with tiny dried flower blossoms and moss.

Arts and crafts stores usually carry many kinds of wreaths. It's worth noting that wreath centerpieces don't have to stand upright. A centerpiece laid flat as a base for flowers and plants, creates a fresh, novel look. (see Appendix, Pages 112; 115-116)

CHAPTER 8

CEREMONY
FOREVER YOURS

Some prefer tradition. Others heed the advice of philosopher Jean Jacques Rousseau, who said, "Take the course opposite to custom and you will almost always do well."

Bird Seed in Designer Flowers

When leaving the church, guests are handed what looks to be a flower. It's actually satin, lace or tulle fabric shaped like a flower. Wrapped inside is bird seed for showering the couple as they exit the church. If it is constructed properly, all guests have to do is shake the "flower" at the couple and send the bird seed en route.

Flower Petal Cones

There is a kinder, gentler alternative to birdseed. Use aromatic flower petals to shower the newlyweds as they exit the church. For the petal container, obtain sheets of either parchment or floral paper. Bend the sheets into cone shapes and glue, tape or place a sticky gold seal on the paper's edge to hold the cone shape. Lastly, fill the cone with the flower petals of choice.

Indoor Vine and Flower Gazebo

A natural-looking gazebo is a rather spectacular and unexpected sight for an indoor wedding. By using brown plastic tubing as the support structure, the four-cornered

41

gazebo is then layered with curly willow, ivy and asparagus fern. Next, place a number of orchids and roses among the greenery. To this natural look, lend an enchanting mood by adding twinkling white lights throughout.

An elaborate indoor gazebo requires several hours prior to the ceremony to construct. So make certain to find a florist who has prior experience in building this kind of gazebo.

Iron Pew

An elegant, antique iron pew for use at the church will set a mood for the ceremony, especially if the wedding is a Victorian one. If a real antique pew cannot be located, contact garden clubs, prop houses, and art stores to obtain a "faux" version of the real thing.

Message with Lots of "Sole" at the Altar

At Catholic ceremonies the groom can make a silent plea for assistance when he kneels down. With the letters HE painted on the bottom of one shoe, and LP on the other, the guests will certainly begin laughing at his call for "HELP." This is one joke that only the groom and possibly the priest know about. But make sure the bride and her family have a healthy sense of humor.

Marriage Bells

These can be real silver bells or bells made of flowers. Hang the bells above the couple as they say the vows. It's even possible, if using real bells, to have them tinkle during that first kiss. Rig them up to a string and have someone pull on them at the propitious moment.

Because Murphy's Law always seems to be operating at times like these, check out the system in advance!

Playbill Programs

This printed wedding program looks just like a playbill for the hottest show on Broadway. Programs make sense for complex ceremonies that contain a variety of elements, such as performances, speakers, songs and invocations.

An elegantly printed program highlights each precious moment as friends and family follow along. It also gives the ushers something to do at the door when greeting incoming guests. If a playbill is too flamboyant for the bride and groom, the programs can be elegantly printed on linen or scrolled paper. Use calligraphy or script-style fonts to add to the presentation. Frame these programs as a keepsake. They'll make a fine addition to the photo album.

Wall of Light

A church filled with guests holding slender, white candles is quite a sight. Pass out the candles to adults as they enter the church. At the beginning of the ceremony have someone important, like a grandparent, use the unity candle to light the first one. Then, one by one, each guest lights the candle of the person sitting next to them. This continues until all the candles have been lit. The ceremony can be coordinated to start at this moment.

To accentuate these candles even more, tie a slender sheath of wheat or a flower to each one, using color-coordinated ribbon.

Unity Candle with an Invitation

Some unity candles are designed so that a message can be affixed to the candle itself. The wedding invitation, for example, is placed onto a carved out section of the candle and covered with a transparent wax for permanent keeping. After the ceremony, move the unity candle to the place-setting table at the reception for all to see.

White Doves

To add a fairy tale touch of fantasy and charm to an outdoor ceremony, get some white doves. Doves can be brought to the ceremony in a gilded cage decorated with white ribbons, bows and flowers. They can be placed just about anywhere if the cage fits into the decor.

Place the doves on each side near the altar, or position them back by the receiving line. Doves, if they are trained, can be released from their cages after the vows are exchanged, at which time they will fly to a predetermined area. However, while this provides a thrilling and romantic impression, remember that animals don't always follow directions.

It's also important to recognize that simply buying doves and letting them fly free is *not* recommended. The reason is a humane one, since cage-raised doves don't survive well on their own. So the most prudent course of action might be to rent two white doves for the day and simply keep them in their cages for all the guests to look at and enjoy.

CHAPTER **9**

DESSERTS
DASHING AND DELIGHTFUL

Wedding cakes are often supplemented with desserts. The
following allow dessert lovers to indulge in sweet fantasies.

Cheesecake Station

There aren't many desserts richer and creamier than
cheesecake. Imaginative caterers will provide everything
from a Snickers bar cheesecake to strawberry cheesecake
and amaretto cheesecake. Top off each slice with a dollop of
whipped cream. *Real* whipped cream. Better to save the fat-
free, cholesterol-free desserts for another day.

Chocolate Station

Since chocolate is reputed to be the "love" drug, this
dessert station might help to spawn a sweet romance. The
nice thing is that it offers a marvelous variety. There's
German chocolate cake, chocolate eclairs, double chocolate
cheesecake, chocolate brownies, chocolate fudge, chocolate
chip cookies, chocolate pound cake, chocolate cream pie,
chocolate-covered strawberries, etc.

Crêpe Station

Guests love to create their own custom creations. A crêpe
station fulfills guests' whims and also lends a touch of
class. The crêpes come hot off the griddle with all kinds of
fillings.

If it's important to appease the health crowd, have the

crêpe station offer whole wheat crêpes—these toast-brown crêpes really are very tasty.

Flambé Station

This popular station is sure to draw a crowd. There's nothing like watching fire meet ice, especially when the result is as luscious as baked Alaska, cherries jubilee flambé, strawberries spumoni flambé, bananas foster flambé and peach melba flambé. Offer assorted varieties of crêpes flambé.

Pie Station

Put the security people on alert because there's likely to be a run on this dessert station. Start out with deep-dish crust pies baked fresh from the oven. Choose from strawberry, rhubarb, blueberry, peach, boysenberry and of course, the all-American apple pie. A la mode is a must.

In addition to offering fruit pies, think about including meringue, pumpkin, pecan, cream pies and even poached pears snuggled in crusty pastry leaves.

Sundae and Frozen Yogurt Station

Introduce a sundae and frozen yogurt station after dinner. Mix in lots of fruit, sprinkles and toppings, hot fudge and whipped cream. Since all the ingredients are present, why not include malts, milk shakes and root beer floats?

46

For the health-minded, stir things up with honey and yogurt shakes. Without a doubt, this dessert station will launch all the ice cream and soft serve frozen yogurt addicts into seventh heaven.

White Wedding Desserts

Here's an array of desserts that will make a heavenly impression upon guests. Start with a creamy white chocolate cheesecake. Include a frothy meringue folded through and through with pecans and a lemon and brandy filling. Try individual servings of a champagne mousse that are as smooth and light as air, and garnished with white grapes that are frosted in sugar. And what about white pound cake with vanilla frosting? The strawberries and whipped cream are optional.

Other tempting white desserts can include a variety of soufflés, puddings and custards—including the popular flan.

CHAPTER 10

FLOWER GIRLS
AND RING BEARERS

When all those sweet "oohs" and "aahs" emanate from the back of the room, it's a sure bet that some darling flower girl is spreading her flower petals and natural charm.

Angel Flower Girl

Looking for something novel for the flower girls? It's simple to transform the little darlings into angels for the processional. All it takes is a halo for them to wear on their heads. (Wings optional.) Decorate the halo with rose petals or roses. Find the halo at a costume house or make one. Remember, there's nothing that says a halo must be round. A heart-shaped halo would be perfect.

Flower Decorated Petal Basket

Here's a way to maximize the beauty of flowers during the ceremony. Have the flower girl sprinkle petals from a basket that is itself completely covered in beautiful flower petals. Using a glue gun and fresh flower blossoms, the basket can be covered in a bands of color. Of course, the basket needs to stored in the fridge after it's completed. Florists can help determine which petals will work best and maintain that truly fresh look.

The Garland Train

When more than one flower girl walks down the aisle, there is sometimes the concern that they won't make it in an orderly fashion. Here's an idea that's both attractive and practical. Have the florist build a long, lush garland consisting of flowers and plants. Attach the front end of the garland to the first flower girl. Then have the others hold onto the sweeping vine. As the leading girl walks forward, the others will be in perfect step. Or as the carnival hawkers are apt to say, "Take one step forward and your body will naturally follow!"

Storybook Characters

The ring bearer and flower girl could be dressed to resemble your favorite storybook characters. Imagine them dressed as a pair, such as Jack and Jill, or Hansel and Gretel. Or each could represent a character from different stories. Either way, they're sure to add a memorable touch to the ceremony.

CHAPTER 11

GARDENS AND BACKYARDS WITH A MAGICAL MOOD

There's nothing like the intimacy of a garden or backyard wedding—especially when the natural surroundings are embellished with an ambiance of serenity and romance.

Carousel

The beauty and magic of a carousel helps makes any setting, especially a backyard one, special. Arrange to have the carousel operated at some point during the reception for the guests to enjoy. Whether guests take a spin or not, the carousel is sure to arouse feelings of joy while making a lasting impression at the same time.

Fountains

The universal appeal of fountains and wishing wells is undeniable. Likewise, a fountain at a backyard wedding can be a focal point where the vows are said. Or, it simply makes for beautiful background ornamentation.

Small fountains can be found at gardens and nurseries, as well as through mail order outlets. As a finishing touch, don't forget to sprinkle some rose petals into the water. For an alternative to a fountain, decorative basins and birdbaths can also add a splash of charm.

Mood-Creating Ornaments

Want to create the feel of pleasure-filled early Rome? Of courtly 18th century France? Of leisurely and refined 19th century England? If so, the answer could be as close as a number of stunning garden ornaments. These ornaments do more than enhance the natural environment. They can help to fashion an ambiance and mood all their own.

Ornaments are available in many materials and shapes: There are terra cotta and limestone statues and sculptures, mini-obelisks, ancient-looking stone columns, weathered bronze sundials, decorative cast iron and stone petal urns, wrought iron fishermen's baskets, a knight's suit of armor, craggy stone troughs and even marble or granite garden tables.

If the authentic item isn't available, do what Hollywood does: Use props found at theatrical rental stores. If stores don't stock a particular item, they might be able to suggest where to find it.

Use some creativity and look beyond nurseries and garden centers to arts and crafts stores. Reproductions of original ornaments can be found in mail order garden catalogs and hobby stores. Several very authentic-looking reproductions, crafted out of fiberglass, cast stone and aluminum, can be found. (see Appendix, Page 115)

Love Seats & Benches

One or more delicately designed, two-seater cast iron benches strategically placed in the garden add to the romance of the moment. These white, cast iron benches can also be placed in the front row, reserved for grandparents or other close family. Cast iron benches come in a variety of intricate floral and pastoral patterns.

There are other styles of benches that can add the needed ambiance. Don't rule out a nice, comfortable wooden bench. Or a swing suspended from a tree. New or old, benches beckon to those wanting to sit in a shady spot, enjoy a cool drink, or have a private conversation.

Bargain benches might be found at swap meets, flea markets and antique shows.

CHAPTER **12**

GUEST BOOK SIGN-IN

Guest sign-in books are nice, but they are all too likely
stuffed away in the back if some cabinet after a few weeks.
Fortunately, this does not have to be the case. The following
ideas will truly involve guests.

Art Canvas

If the guest list includes an artistic crowd, a stretched
canvas is an interesting alternative to a guest book. Place a
stretched canvas on an easel at the reception. Make
available a variety of brushes, squeeze tubes of glitter,
paints, colored markers and even rubber stamps. It might

help if the canvas has some background or design on it to begin with. This will help to start things off and provide a motif others can add to.

To avoid those unsightly accidents, remember to use washable, water-soluble paints and markers.

Christmas Tree Skirt

This idea is perfect for a Christmas wedding. Instead of a guest book, have guests sign their names on the bride and groom's Christmas tree skirt. The tree skirt will provide extra meaning and festive memories to each succeeding Christmas as it's placed on the tree.

Fantastic Fabric

Long a tradition at Chinese weddings, the idea of having guests sign a fabric which is later transformed into a wall hanging can be adapted to any wedding celebration. Swaths of fabric can be placed on a table at the reception, along with indelible ink pens. The 'scripted' fabric can later be framed or stitched together to create a keepsake pillow cover or quilt. (see Appendix, Pages 111-113)

Jigsaw Puzzle

Yes, you read that correctly—a jigsaw puzzle. Actually, the guests will sign on the back of individual pieces of the puzzle. But then this isn't just *any* jigsaw puzzle. It's one that's made from a photo of the bride and groom. There are companies that will do this. That means providing them with a negative, in either 35mm film or larger format. Typically, the larger negative produces larger jigsaw puzzles and sharper photo images.

Set the pieces near the place setting cards so guests can sign them as they enter the reception. Leave the pieces on the table so that later, guests can piece the puzzle together. The picture on the jigsaw puzzle could represent a shared, candid moment between the bride and groom or even a formal photo.

Memory Lane Guest Book

This guest book will feature more than names. Similar to the Memory Album (see Chapter 19), each guest will be asked to write down a memory of the bride and groom. This memory could be the first time the guest met the couple, a favorite memory, or a humorous memory. To make these memories come alive, guests could be asked to bring along any mementos from the remembered event, including everything from newspaper clippings and appointment book calendars to ticket stubs and photos. The resulting guest book is a vivid trip down memory lane that will have added significance in the years to come.

CHAPTER 13

INVITATIONS
INVENTIVE AND INNOVATIVE

Invitations needn't be so formal. Here are alternatives that will make the first impression a lasting one.

3-Dimensional Invitation

This invitation is 3-D in the sense that it's not flat. It's really a beautifully designed collage of elements that are glued on to the front of the invitation. The effect could be to create an elaborate, miniaturized bouquet made of flowers, tulle, lace and pearls.

By using a fabric stiffener, lace and other fabrics can be molded to resemble fans or other objects. Another idea?—

press flowers to create original designs similar to Japanese flower water-color paintings and create a work of art that is a real keepsake. (see Appendix, Page 115)

Caricature Invitation

Have an artist draw up caricatures of the bride and groom dressed in wedding gown and tuxedo. They could be portrayed with their arms outstretched and fingers pointing at the reader with the caption "We want YOU!!!...." Upon opening the card, the guests get the rest of the message: "...To attend our wedding and have a great time!" A pen and ink drawing will provide better quality than a pencil caricature. In order to comply with printing requirements, be sure to tell the printer what's being planned.

Fairy Tale Invitation

Who says Cinderella doesn't live today? One couple actually created a four-page fold-out, story book, or fairy tale, style invitation. Using both pictures and words, the brief story traced the story of the little boy and girl who grew into adulthood, eventually met and fell in love. The fairy tale ended happily by telling the guests where the wedding took place. It even told how all the honored guests had a joyful, merry time of drinking and dancing at the reception!

Using the story book idea as a starting point, there are a number of imaginative directions in which to go. If the bride and groom stick with the fairy tale concept, they could use "old English" or colloquial language to make the invitations distinct. Existing fairy tales can be modified to match any situation. Check out some books of fairy tales for more ideas.

While custom story book invitations are usually more expensive than buying pre-designed invitations, they are not necessarily a lot more costly if there are friends or associates who can help. The bride and groom may have a friend who is a graphic artist. Perhaps there's someone at the workplace who produces the company newsletter. With a little help, custom invitations can be designed for a reasonable price.

Handmade Paper Invitation

Handmade papers can be utilized as borders, paper-parchment folders or in a number of intriguing ways. These papers come in a variety of styles, each possessing its own distinctive elements. For example, floral paper expresses a romantic feeling; glitter paper glimmers with a fun, contemporary look; parfait paper creates a sophisticated, refined impression. There is even a natural handmade paper that yields a gentle, holistic impression.

Because handmade paper must be individually made, each invitation is, by definition, one-of-a-kind. (see Appendix, Page 119)

Photographic Invitation

Remember those Christmas greeting cards with photos of the family on them? Well, a similar card style can be done for wedding invitations. Get a good portrait artist to do a photo of the bride and groom either alone or with their families. Then, have this photo transferred to the front of the invitation.

Poetry Invitation

Create something unique that works within the more traditional wedding invitation format. Do the bride and groom have a favorite short poem or song? Writer and poet Kahil Gibran's books of poems are quite moving. Shakespeare mused about the power of love in many of his plays. It could be quite a fun project finding a poem that expresses what the couple feels.

Whether the poem is original or found, a poem can easily be incorporated into the invitation. When thinking about which poem to use, remember the words of Ralph Waldo Emerson, who said, "The quality of the imagination is to flow and not to freeze." So have fun finding the words that express your feelings!

Silhouette Invitation

Here's an invitation idea that is different and very personal. A silhouette artist draws a profile and then cuts it out on a dark sheet of paper. The resulting framed silhouette resembles a cameo pendant.

Also, a bride and groom can have their finished silhouettes used as artwork for the front of their invitations. To make these invitations really shine, have the silhouettes embossed or done on glossy foil paper.

Stenciled Invitation

Stencils can be used to make even a plain card look stunning. A variety of stencils can be found in art stores, or they can easily be made and cut out. Think about using such things as glitter, metallic spray paint and colored inks to accent a design or spell out a message on the front of the invitation.

In addition, stenciling can be combined with handmade papers to create a striking, exotic invitation that reinforces the wedding's theme and style.

Very Victorian Invitation

For a one-of-a-kind invitation, go to swap meets and estate sales, and locate original Victorian wallpaper or engravings. After that, it's a simple matter to take these exquisite designs and images to the printer to have them printed onto the invitations.

Be flexible, and place these images where they seem to fit best—either as a border, a background, or part of the central design.

CHAPTER 14

LOCATIONS AND SITES SENSATIONAL

Couples can get married in almost any place imaginable—although some might shudder at the thought. In alphabetical order, here are the ABCs of locations...

I Didn't Know I Could Get Married There!

An *Aquarium, Arboretum* or *Auditorium,* a *Ballroom, Barn* or *Beach,* a *Castle, Chapel, Church* or *Courthouse,* a *Dam* (Hoover's), an *Eatery,* a *Farmhouse,* a *Gazebo,* a *Hacienda,* an *Indian Reserve,* a *Japanese Garden,* a *Knoll, Las Vegas,* a *Meadow* or *Museum,* a *National (State & City) Park,* an *Orange Grove,* a *Presidential Library,* the *Queen Mary,* a *Rose Garden,* a *Saloon, Salon* or *Spanish Mission,* a *Theme Park* or *Train,* a *Union Hall,* a *Victorian Home,* a *Winery,* a *X-mas Day in the home,* a *Yacht,* a *Zoo.*

How does one find these locations? Actually, it's pretty easy. First, most cities will provide a list of wedding sites. Just call the local chamber of commerce or the department of parks and recreation. Usually, they will provide most of the information needed, including equipment availability, maps, access, permits and costs.

Visit the local library and delve into the National Register of Historical Places to find presidential museums, Victorian homes and other unusual locations. If there's a special place of interest, give them a call. Another valuable source is a book called *Places.* It's available at most libraries.

Then there are places *not* to get married. If you're considering the following sites, you might want to think things over before sending out those invitations: An

Assembly line, a *Barracks*, a *Car*, *Cemetery*, or *Closet*, a *Dock*, an *Elevator*, a *Fast Food Restaurant* or *Ferris Wheel*, a *Greenhouse*, a *Hospital*, an *Ice Rink*, a *Jail*, a *Kiosk*, a *Liquor Store*, a *Monastery*, the *North Pole*, an *Oil Field*, a *Pawnshop*, a *Quiz Show*, a *Retail Clothing Store*, a *Service Station*, *Tut's Tomb*, *Underground,* a *Vault*, a *Washroom*, *Weight Room*, or *Woodshed*, a *Xerox Room*, a *Yogurt Shop*, a *Zoo.*

CHAPTER 15

MUSIC AND ENTERTAINMENT

A wedding encompasses many of the same components as a musical production. There is a director (wedding planner), the lead players (bride and groom), the cast (bridal party), and musicians (band, DJ). Here is a collection of supporting players who can add extra pizazz.

Barbershop Quartet

The four-part sound texture of barbershop quartets can be traced back to the 15th century. But its popularity in the United States stems from the old-fashioned, romantic nature of the songs and their gorgeous harmonies. Consider a barbershop quartet as additional entertainment before the ceremony or during the regular band's intermission. Watch as the older guests glow and reminisce, while the younger guests marvel at the innocence and beauty of these venerable tunes.

Bubbles, Tiny Bubbles

As the reception gets under way, turn down the lights and turn on the bubble machine. Bubbles will float around the dance floor as the bride and groom share their first dance. In addition to renting a bubble machine, bubble blowers can be placed at each table so the guests can join in on the fun.

Caricature Artist

Caricature artists will flatter guests by putting their faces and favorite hobbies on sketch pads. These artists can be hired for three to four hours during the reception. Set them up in the corner and they'll delight everyone, including the bride and groom, with their wild and crazy interpretations of the wedding.

Celebrity Look-Alike

If the bride and groom are politically oriented, hiring a celebrity Presidential look-alike to make a toast could be a real hoot. If possible, plan this without the knowledge of the bride and groom. Imagine their surprise when the lights dim and an announcement is made that a special VIP guest is arriving to make a short visit! When *You're A Grand Old Flag* or other patriotic song begins to play, they'll wonder what in the world is going on. The celebrity look-alike could also be a favorite movie star or other favorite character.

Christmas Carolers

To make any Christmas wedding truly an extension of the holiday, bring in a group of carolers to sing Christmas carols as guests arrive for dinner. With the lights dimmed and singing by candle light, carolers will help bring the spirit of Christmas to life for all those who are present.

Karaoke

Karaoke has caught on to the extent where some people are using this fun sing-along device at weddings. Those DJs who have karaoke equipment include it for an extra charge. Like Tom Cruise in *Top Gun*, the groom can sing his favorite tune to his beloved, only this time with full musical accompaniment. Not every DJ offers karaoke, so ask in advance. Some DJ set-ups are so elaborate that they offer strobe and laser lighting.

Magician

Magicians who specialize in close-up magic add a certain sparkle to the entertainment provided by the band. Magicians can entertain during the band's intermission, using the bride and groom as willing subjects. Afterwards, have the magician stroll around the room, amazing guests with sleight of hand and comedy routines.

Mariachi Band

Latin lovers aren't the only ones who enjoy the truly romantic and passionate music of the mariachis. Roving from table to table, a mariachi band will add a musical flair to almost any party. The band can stroll the floor as guests enter the reception hall. Best of all, when the bride and groom enter the room, the band can play them a special song, such as *Bésame Mucho*. Guests will be sure to remember and appreciate this wonderful musical treat long after the last note is played.

Multi-Image Show

Combine a montage of visual images with music to tell a story and entertain, and the result is called multi-image. Typically, it utilizes two or three slide projectors (sometimes more) to project a large number of photographic slide images onto an oversized screen. The images are choreographed to musical selections to make for an emotional and fun presentation.

Multi-image can be incorporated into a wedding with great success. Imagine walking into the reception hall to a multi-image presentation showing the bride and groom as babies. The guests witness them grow and mature from cuddly childhood into gawky adolescence.

Finally, there comes a picture of the two of them together. The audience sees the two lives converging as one. And of course, the show can feature humorous text, titles and commentary along the way. Once completed, a multi-image presentation—with all its visuals and music combined— can be transferred onto videotape. Some videographers, as well as production companies, offer this added service.

Rock Around the Clock

Bring on the Fonz! Classic jukeboxes add a real flavor to a '50s style wedding. But then again, it's hard not to fall in love with jukeboxes stocked with golden oldies and the bride and groom's own favorite songs.

Use the jukebox as a fun interlude during the band's intermission or to provide all the music. Newer Wurlitzer jukeboxes even provide CD digital sound quality. The bride and groom can buy a jukebox, but unless they plan to keep it, renting is probably the best option. (see Appendix, Page 122)

Santa Claus

A Christmas wedding with Santa as a special visitor might provide the perfect time for Santa to hand out the party favors in person to all the good boys, girls and guests. After handing out the gifts—at a predetermined station or by going table to table—Santa could spend some time with the children and even lead everyone in a chorus of *Jingle Bells*.

Square Dance Caller

For about the same cost of a mobile DJ, it's possible to hire a Square Dance Caller who will bring his own equipment and also serve as emcee. A good caller keeps the party hopping by teaching the guests how to square dance. It's a wonderful way to get the guests to mix.

If the bride and groom want some variety, request that the caller bring some additional waltz or other music from his/her collection. Many callers will also teach guests how to do popular line dances.

Steel Drum Band

Steel drums make for great dance music, tailor-made for an outdoor wedding, either at a park or near the beach. Wait until guests hear rock and roll, soul or a slow dance on those reverberating steel drums.

However, if there's a theme wedding, get a band to match that particular theme. (see Chapter 22, Themes)

CHAPTER 16

PARTY FAVORS
IN MANY FLAVORS

Party favors take many forms and cover the range from extravagant to modest. Best of all, they offer the opportunity to create something personal and memorable that expresses thanks to guests for sharing in the bride and groom's joy.

Bride and Groom Chocolate Coins

For a party favor to place on each table, here's a really rich idea: Chocolate or chocolate mint coins. But not just any coins. These coins feature sculptured likenesses of the bride and groom. Get a confectioner to design the molds and make them out of milk chocolate. And since the bride and groom are the treasury department, they can "mint" themselves into any denomination.

Christmas Tree Ornaments

If the wedding is near or around Christmas time, then a personalized Christmas tree ornament makes a practical and thoughtful favor. The ornaments can be shaped like angels, stars, spheres or imprinted with names of the bride and groom. (see Appendix, Page 119)

Color Coordinated Candies

Why not enhance your wedding's color design with tasty candies to match? Some confectioners will make candies in custom colors. And, there are candy-making kits that the do-it-yourselfer can use with the right ingredients and food coloring to achieve the same effect.

Another alternative? Make the party favor holders out of color coordinated fabrics in a variety of shapes and designs. Imagine, for example, a buttercup-shaped tulle favor holder. Perhaps a shimmering, heart-shaped favor holder made of satin would add that extra touch of style and glamour. And don't forget ribbons, which are available in a rainbow of colors just waiting to accent party favor packaging.

Cookie Cutters

Believe it or not, cookie cutters can be transformed into wedding favors. First, fill the cookie cutters with a variety of little Valentine candies, chocolates or nuts. After wrapping up the whole concoction in a sheer material or fine net, simply plunk on a bow. Heart-shaped cookie cutters are perfect for weddings.

Flower Power

Tie a flower, such as a chrysanthemum, orchid, or rose, onto a ribbon. As guests enter for the ceremony, they receive the flower favor to affix to their jacket or dress. They can then wear this colorful adornment throughout the reception.

74

Fortune Cookies

One solid prediction is that fortune cookie favors will be appreciated and remembered by guests. Each fortune could be imprinted with the bride and groom's names and date of the wedding. Or mix in several pithy messages such as "You will attend a wild party," "We really did it," or "Your love warms those close to you." For fun, throw in the occasional message that pleads, "Help me—I'm a slave in a fortune cookie factory!"

Guitar Picks for Music Lovers

This fun, personalized favor is ideal for bride and grooms who are musicians or for those who simply want to share their appreciation of music. Some suppliers of guitar picks will imprint the names of the bride and groom right on guitar picks. If there's room, include the wedding date. For musicians who get married and invite their musician friends, this is a practical party favor that will be used and enjoyed time and time again.

Humorous Novelty Favors

Novelty favors are for the bride and groom who are known for having a sense of humor. There are a number of funny knickknacks that guests can wind up, squeeze or poke at. A trip to the local novelty store or costume house should produce the right humorous favor to tickle the funny bone.

Inspirational Note Cards

Promises. Trust. Wisdom. Faith. Unconditional love. Acceptance. Persistence. Comfort. Each of these words holds a special significance that can be imparted to guests in a meaningful way. All that's needed are some stationery note cards, calligraphy and imagination. The bride and groom must make a list of words that possess special meaning for them. This can be lots of fun, and even friends and family can "donate" special words. A single word is then written on the inside of the note cards.

As a nice touch, tie the note card closed with some gold string or ribbon. Here are some other inspirational words: Compassion. Tolerance. Unity. Empathy. Understanding. Rapture. Patience. Forgiveness. Commitment. Joy.

Lottery Tickets

Include a dollar "scratcher" lottery ticket with each of the guest's party favors. This will be a good conversation piece for years to come. If it's in the budget, buy a few extra tickets for the band members.

Matchbook with Calculator

Electronic gadgetry has become so miniaturized that even tiny calculators can fit behind a matchbook cover. The matchbook, which is inscribed with the names of the bride and groom and date of the wedding, houses the calculator. It's a good calculation that this compact and useful party favor will both amaze and delight guests.

Matchbook with Notepad

Although less flashy than a mini-calculator, at least this matchbook is useful in its own way. The mini-pad makes it easy to jot notes down and will almost certainly find its way to many a guest's work desk.

Perfume and Cologne Bottles

Actually, this goes under the category of *extravagant* party favors. Have favorite perfume and cologne fragrances bottled in containers engraved with the names of the bride and groom. Guests will appreciate this useful and attractive party favor.

Personalized Paperweight (See Place Cards)

A paperweight favor will hold down memories as well as papers. Some hobby and art stores sell molds for making paperweights. Fill the mold with a clear plastic such as Lucite, then add individual letters strung like beads to spell out the name of the guest or any other message. Sparkle things up by mixing in some glitter and confetti.

Phone Cards

In today's communications-crazed world, picture the surprise of guests who open that slim envelope at their table setting and find a phone card inside. Phone cards are not only practical, they're as good as money and are relatively inexpensive.

Phone cards are purchased by the amount of time available on the card—usually in blocks of thirty minutes or one hour. Best of all, the bride and groom will fondly thought of as guests dial up a relative, friend or loved one to spread the word about the fantastic wedding they attended. These cards can even be customized with the names of the bride and groom.

Picture Frames (See Place Cards)

Miniature picture frames come in all styles and can be found from high quality stationery stores to the five-and-ten. These could double as place card settings by inserting the names of guests and their table numbers inside. This practical favor is a nice remembrance that guests will be able to use around the house or office. (Appendix, Page 120)

Sachet with Potpourri

Here's a pretty, yet practical party favor which guests will want to take home with them. Embroider the lucky bride and groom's names, along with the wedding date, on a sachet. After filling it with the sweet scents of potpourri, tie the end with a satin or lace ribbon. For an added touch of elegance, loosely wrap a strand of baby pearls around the bag.

Stationery Holders

Have the local jeweler engrave the names or initials of each guest on silver stationery pad holders. To really get noticed and remembered, apply this personal touch to a Tiffany. It's guaranteed everyone will want to be invited to the bride and groom's next party.

Sterling Silver Picture Frames

Here's an idea fit for a President. No kidding, since this party favor was used at a celebration dinner for then President-elect Clinton after his successful 1992 campaign. It begins with exquisite 3 1/2" x 5" sterling silver or silver-plated picture frames. Every couple has a frame waiting when they sit down for dinner. Then, all of the couples are photographed on 35mm film which is processed at a one hour lab. Arrange in advance to have the lab open during the dinner. After processing, photos are rushed back and placed in the proper frames so the guests can take them home.

Because of the logistics and coordination, make sure there are enough photographers to shoot film and keep track of which prints go where.

Wedding Cake Boxes

As guests depart, leave them with an exquisite box tied closed with a fine golden thread. Inside—place a slice of the wedding cake to enjoy later in the evening or with coffee the next morning.

Welcome Baskets

Out-of-town guests have gone out of their way to be at the wedding. So why not pleasantly surprise them when they arrive at the hotel or home? (No, don't hide behind the door and shout "surprise!" when they walk in.) Instead, greet them with a welcome basket loaded with lots of fresh fruit and snacks. Include a bottle of champagne or a bottle of the guest's favorite wine.

There are many other items that can be placed in the basket. For instance, include a disposable camera for them to bring along to the reception for picture taking. Tuck in some fresh flowers or complimentary tickets for drinks.

Don't forget to include a map of the city, an itinerary, important phone numbers and all other local directions. No-one knows the guests better than the bride and groom. So provide whatever will make guests feel welcome. (see Appendix, Page 119)

CHAPTER 17

PHOTOGRAPHY WITH PANACHE

Wedding photographers are often heard to comment, "Your wedding lasts one day, but your photography lasts forever." Here are some more creative photography ideas.

Black-and-White Photography

What do Ansel Adams' famous nature photographs and Orson Welles' *Citizen Kane* have in common? Black-and-white photography. There's something elegant, indelible and enduring about it. The bride and groom need not have their whole wedding shot in black-and-white, but could arrange to have only certain formals shot that way.

Looking for a more unusual idea?—shoot black-and-white period piece photos of the bride and groom in Victorian attire.

Boudoir Photography

Boudoir photography has come out of the closet and into the bedroom. In addition to taking traditional formals, some photographers will shoot boudoir photographs as a sexy, unique surprise gift for the groom. This is probably most economical if the wedding photographer can include these photos as part of the package.

However, not every wedding photographer is either comfortable and adept at shooting boudoir photography. On the other hand, some photographers already have all the props that will make boudoir photos special, such as antique claw-foot bathtubs and bronze bed posts.

Disposable Cameras

Provide each table with a disposable camera. These nifty cameras even come with different lenses, from portrait to wide-angle. They can even be personalized with the names of the bride and groom.

Disposable cameras get everyone into the mood, and best of all, the guests will snap some real candid photos using this method. However, the use of disposable cameras is best done at the reception rather than the ceremony, since the flashing of multiple cameras could disrupt the vows. One more tip—provide a note at each table reminding the guests to leave the disposable camera on the table or to place it in a basket which is placed near the door.

Hand-Painted Photographic Portraits

This is a process of hand painting on black-and-white photographs with oil paints. The effect usually works best when photos are developed on fiber mat paper, using a low black-and-white contrast. The result can be either a subtle or dramatic portrait that is suitable for framing.

Ask a local black-and-white photo lab for names of colorists. Or take a class and learn this fun hobby.

Photojournalism

Formal and staged photography only depicts one side of a wedding. A photojournalistic style provides a more candid perspective. Through the use of long lenses capable of taking pictures from across the room, the story of a wedding is told through close-ups and by catching on film those beautiful, spontaneous moments that might otherwise be lost.

Wedding photojournalism makes for a nice addition to traditional wedding photography. A single photographer can't do both of these styles at the same time. So make sure that the photographers coordinate their efforts and know how to avoid showing up in each other's pictures!

Snapshots in an Instant

Using Polaroids to get quick pictures of guests is easy. Simply buy square, card-like folders and have an album company stamp them in advance with the name of the party and the wedding date.

Have the photographer use an SX70 Polaroid camera to produce square pictures that fit into the folders. Photos can be taken right at the table or at a designated "photo center" located nearby or in the reception hall.

CHAPTER 18

PLACE CARDS

Place cards are like the parsley at the side of the food. Boring, ignored and unimaginative. Fight the boredom with these attention-getting ideas.

Bookmark Place Card

Here's a unique place card that doubles as a bookmark. Laminated for extra durability, the card includes the guest's name engraved or imprinted on it. If desired, the reverse side of the card can also include the couple's name, a line of poetry, or date of the wedding. Lastly, the card is tastefully adorned with a tassel which is looped through and tied at one end of the bookmark.

Cute as a Button

Instead of the traditional place card, offer custom pin-on buttons. Like the popular buttons of the sixties and seventies, these buttons can have almost any print, design or message written on them. Consider a design that places the bride and groom's names around the edges. Then, smack dab in the center, place the guest's name and their table number written in calligraphy or script style.

Craft and hobby stores might have what's needed to make these specialty items. Or check out mail order hobby catalogs. In addition, some advertising agencies can get buttons made to order.

Edible Place Cards

Just about everything else is edible these days, so why not place cards? We're talking about delicate place cards made out of sugar. Guests' names can be scribed in a color of choice, and the cards themselves can be decorated any way. They'll last, too. That is, unless they're eaten first.

Personalized Paperweight (See Party Favors)

While making personalized paperweight place cards is labor intensive, it's a thoughtful gift that will be appreciated. Molds and clear plastic filler can be found at hobby and art stores. This detailed job also requires arranging all of the alphanumeric beads to spell out the names and table numbers. Don't forget to include some glitter and colored confetti to complete this distinctive and long-lasting place card.

Picture Frames (See Party Favors)

This is a real frame up! Just buy small picture frames— they can be purchased at most stationery stores—and insert guests' names and table numbers. Best of all, these frames double as a practical party favor. Some mail order stores specialize in frames. (see Appendix, Page 120)

CHAPTER 19

RECEPTIONS TO REMEMBER

Receptions are the height of joy and festivity. Accentuate the mood because it's definitely party time!

Balloon Sculpture and Decoration

Balloons of both latex and mylar offer a variety of looks and colors. Balloons can be sculptured to create almost any shape or design imaginable, from canopies and pillars to columns and arches by the head table.

Guests can enter the reception hall through a heart-shaped balloon sculpture. Or, how about a magnificent balloon sculpture of a rose floating above the bride and groom? In addition, think about all those things that can be placed *inside* a balloon. Like champagne, flower bouquets and even chocolates.

Streamers and confetti add yet another dimension to the decorative balloons. Finally, instead of matchbooks, print a custom message or the names of the bride and groom on the balloons. Just make sure to check all pins at the door.

Names of balloon designers and decorators can be found in the Yellow Pages.

Candle of Many Colors

Here's something that is both beautiful and meaningful. Create a unique vows candle by filling an antique glass with brightly colored glass chips or aquarium pebbles. Place a small votive candle in the center of the colored pieces. Such a multi-colored candle can be placed on the head table or as decoration throughout the reception hall.

Chairs with Chutzpah

How can flair and romance be added to the reception hall? What draws all eyes to the bride and groom at the front of the room, yet is a simple enough to be done quickly and without great cost? The answer: Decorating the chairs of the bride and groom.

Consider using little bouquets or clusters of flowers with a fern or ivy background. As a finishing touch, add in some well positioned tulle or colored bows. There's also a helium balloon sculpture, as mentioned above, which could rise high above the chairs.

Collage Presentation

Take an oversized picture frame, and create a collage of photos of the bride and groom growing up individually, then together. Include funny shots and even little notes and cards that they saved and may have written to one another. This touching collage will tell the story of how their two lives became one. Place the collage on the gift table or hang it where it will be viewed.

Commemorative Plate

Decorative plates have become popular collectibles. They're even traded through exchanges, much like any stock exchange. But the bride and groom don't need to have a limited edition plate to get their name, likeness and other particulars painted on one. Place the bride and groom's personalized commemorative plate at the head table or on display where guests enter the reception. (see Appendix, Page 111)

Fans and Lace

Giant pleated fans can be used to decorate buffet or hors d'oeuvre tables. These can be covered with sheer lace, or as a special touch, the vows or a favorite poem can be written onto the fans. To further enhance the buffet table, drape lengths of lace or another fabric on the front of the buffet table.

Giant Hearts

Six foot high hearts made out of canvas can be hung from the ceiling of the reception hall. The hearts, which are painted red and decorated with satin or glitter trimming, make quite a visual image. If the wedding is held on Valentine's Day, the hearts will tie into the romantic theme of the day.

Memory Album

Here's looking at you, bride and groom! Place a photo album on a reception table and ask people to write their favorite memories of the bride and groom onto the scrap pages. The memory album can also be passed around in an impromptu fashion. As an added touch, place photos of the bride and groom throughout the book. Guests can also bring candid photos for the book. Just write a note on the reverse of the invitation asking them to bring their best or funniest photos for use in a memory album. (see Appendix, Pages 120; 123)

Mementos Box

Ask guests to bring souvenirs to the wedding. These may be photos from high school, college or almost anything that recalls a sweet memory. Place the box where all guests will see it when they arrive.

For the mementos box, use a finely appointed hat box or a dainty Victorian Keepsake Box—preferably heart-shaped—that has been decorated with lace, flowers and ribbon. These boxes are often painted or porcelainized.

As with the memory album, a note requesting mementos can be written on the invitation.

Movie Posters

Do the bride and groom want to star in their own production? If so, consider showcasing the bride and groom in their own "one sheet" or poster like those used in the movies. Use ideas from classic movie posters. Then have a photographer take a posed shot and compose a headline to add in later. Use an existing favorite film like *Casablanca*, or humorous titles like *The Love That Grew and Grew and Grew* or *Love Story XV*. Some print shops, ad agencies or artistic friends can help. Many quick-print shops offer color xerography that can enlarge photos to poster size for a very nominal cost.

Twinkling Lights

Place twinkling Christmas lights—the battery operated kind—strategically on and around each table's centerpiece, along the head table, in flower arrangements and just about anywhere that makes aesthetic sense. The delicate lights will brighten up floral arrangements and send the message that it definitely 'tis the season to be merry! This decor makes a Christmas wedding brighten with joy.

Wedding Plaque

Use imagination to create this decoration and keepsake. Although plaques can be made out of almost any material, the local ceramic shop can construct the wedding plaque. Plaques can contain the names of the bride and groom, interlocking hearts and the wedding date. Then hang the wedding plaque from the head table or at the place card table.

CHAPTER 20

REGISTRIES MADE TO ORDER

From the ordinary to the unorthodox, there are registries for almost every taste.

Home, Hardware and More

With so many couples getting married later in life, the types of gifts they need have changed greatly. For example, couples moving into their first home might find it helpful to register with a hardware store. Those couples into building up an audio and video collection can register at a music store or video store.

In addition, consider stores that specialize in arts and crafts, computers, electronics, gardens, health, sporting goods and nature/earth. The key is to let needs and desires dictate registry choices.

Mail Order

There are lots of great mail order catalogs around, and many of them accommodate registries. Try museum shops, such as New York's *Museum of Modern Art*. They offer a large variety of kitchen, home and art items. For the rugged, outdoor types, there are *Land's End* and *Eddie Bauer*.

There's also the nationwide jeweler and catalog store, *Service Merchandise*. Their computerized bridal network keeps track of gifts, making shopping easy for friends and family wherever they may live. And the store offers some 10,000 items. (see Appendix, Page 118)

Remember, even if a store doesn't normally have a bridal registry it may still be able to help. It's worth asking.

CHAPTER 21

TABLES
AND TABLE SETTINGS

Table decoration is an art. Here are several ideas that add flair to any table setting.

Cake Look-Alike Sweet Table

The ultimate sweet table actually looks like a three-tier cake! Start with a basic round table. From the top edge of the table, hang a cardboard skirt which should reach down

to the ground. Paint the top to resemble icing dripping over the edge of the cake. On the lower half of the skirt, paint sprinkles of color or balloons. To build the second tier, place a large circular stand in the center of the table and decorate it with a painted skirt. On top of this, set an even smaller lazy Susan tray with a painted cake skirt. With the festive three-tier "cake" table finished, arrange luscious desserts on the various levels.

Champagne Glasses

Surprise the bride and groom by having personalized champagne glasses at the head table. First names or family initials will do nicely. These could be provided for the whole head table as keepsakes. Industrious-minded brides and grooms can find glass etching kits and have the satisfaction of being able to say "I did that." Certain stores provide this service. (see Appendix, Page 122)

Ivy Napkin Holders

Make napkin rings out of ivy. Then place a rose or other flower inside with the napkin. Another possibility? Obtain or make tasseled napkin rings in almost any color. These tassels, combined with matching tablecloths and linens, make for finely appointed and coordinated tables.

Holiday Garlands

Festive garlands, the color of choice, are distributed around the centerpiece. This is especially suitable for Christmas weddings, with bright red or green garlands adding a dash of holiday cheer. For a traditional Christmas flair, add red ribbons and blossoming, freshly cut sprigs of holly.

Heather Napkin Holders

If a splash of color is preferred, consider heather napkin holders. The evergreen leaves and delicate flower clusters of pink-purple make an attractive holder. Adding some sheer lace makes for a more delicate look.

Monogrammed Linen, Napkin or Porcelain

Here's the ultimate in chic and élan. Monogrammed initials make a powerful statement about the importance of the family name. Initials can be emblazoned onto porcelain coffee cups or stitched onto the linen.

Personalized Lobster Bibs

For lucky guests who are treated to the *real thing* —boiled lobster in the shell, crab and other foods not easily eaten with just a fork and knife—brighten up the reception and table settings with personalized lobster bibs. To do this, place the bibs over chairs of those guests eating the meal. Finding a bib with their name on it will make guests feel special. And it will make that lobster dinner even more memorable.

A Picture Worth a Thousand Numbers

The first thing most people do when arriving at a reception is to find out which table they're seated at. Then comes searching out the numbers that poke up from the center of each table. For those who always wished there was a more original way, here it is: Simply replace those number cards with pictures or photographs.

The use of pictures can tie in nicely with a theme. For example, have card-sized photos of favorite movie stars at each table. Imagine the guests' surprise at discovering they are sitting at the Marilyn Monroe table. Or the Clark Gable table. What the heck, why not use today's big name stars. Rock and rollers. Comedians. Geniuses.

Table photographs can also express wedding themes. For example, a Roaring Twenties Theme could feature tables for flappers, player pianos, whiskey stills and famous persons of that era. Sports fans could have names of their favorite sports teams and players. Film buffs could have tables tied in to their favorite movie. Those cards representing tables can be almost anything. So have fun and go for it!

Table Skirt Decorations

Beautiful ribbons hand-painted in wedding colors can adorn the skirt of a tablecloth. These can be pinned four or six ribbons to a table, tucking up the skirt where it hangs over the edge of the table. The result? The linen edge scallops up around the bottom, rather than forming a straight line as it hangs down. If something a bit more ornate is wanted, add a few green silk or real leaves to the ribbons.

Victorian (Figurine) Napkin Rings

From the mid 19th through the early 20th century, silver napkin rings featuring figurines were produced by the thousands. The dainty, sculpted figures included cherubs, little boys and girls, a variety of flowers, and a menagerie of birds, horses and squirrels—even butterflies. Today, these napkin rings are antiques. Yet the effort in finding them will be rewarded by bringing back the days when table setting truly was an art form. Some stores offer a classical version of the original. (see Appendix, Page 115)

CHAPTER 22

THEMES
TO MATCH YOUR DREAMS

Here are eighteen unforgettable themes to try on for size:

Ante-bellum Theme

The ante-bellum, which refers to that time before the U.S. Civil War, harkens back to the old South. This wedding will best emphasize a time known for its genteel charm, grand style, distinguished music, distinctive attire and exquisite cuisine.

Bluegrass/Country Western Theme

Get ready to pull out the old fiddle, stomp your feet and put on cowboy hats. Some couples even have formal photos shot in full western attire. In keeping with the theme, there's nothing like a family-style barbecue to get things rolling. If the guests want, they might slip into jeans for the reception.

Futuristic Theme

With a futuristic theme, guests can take part in the "wedding of tomorrow." The journey begins when guests pick up their pin-on name cards—aptly shaped like those "communicators" seen on *Star Trek*. Next, guests enter a "time transport tunnel" of flashing lights and hear a recorded message telling them how to prepare for their trip into the 23rd century. The tunnel is actually a decorated doorway or hallway leading into the reception. An usher or actor dressed as an Interstellar Guide welcomes the time traveling guests.

As for designing the reception, the future could be as far out as desired. The party could even take place on the bridge of *Star Trek's* celebrated starship Enterprise and include visiting relatives—the Klingons and Vulcans!

Gangster-Moll Theme

The myth of gangsters, perpetuated in real life by the likes of Al Capone and Bonnie and Clyde, continues to capture the imagination. Instead of a number, each table could feature the name of a various former gangster. Swing music, an antique gin mill and other popular icons of that era would be incorporated into the decorations.

Halloween/Costume Theme

If costumes are the central theme, then this wedding needn't be held on Halloween. However, balloons and other Halloween style decorations and centerpieces will make this memorable. One caveat: It's advisable that only one couple come dressed as a bride and groom!

Hawaiian Luau Theme

Ever been to a Hawaiian barbecue? Typically found are pineapples carved out and filled with drinks, Hawaiian leis, grass hula skirts and lots of dancing.

Midnight Wedding Theme

The adventurous, the romantic and the sleepless go where others fear to tread. For those who dare to be different, imagine a candlelight ceremony taking place as the clock strikes the midnight hour. If the bride and groom—and their guests—are prepared to party till dawn, then this is the way to go. Consider a romantic candle light dinner or a buffet.

The unusual timing of the wedding will require certain accommodations from wedding vendors, but the result will be memorable as guests dance to *Rock Around the Clock*—literally!

Movie or Book Theme

The bride and groom could be Rhett Butler and Scarlett O'Hara at a *Gone With the Wind* theme wedding. Or they could vault into the next century and *Star Wars*.

Pick the movie and characters of choice or go one better and have an "Oscars" theme wedding, complete with "Best Actress" and "Best Actor" awards presented to the bride and groom. It's also an opportunity to give credit to those who starred as "Best Supporting" friends and family. Naturally, everyone will want to win as "Best Director"!

Murder Mystery Theme

This may be the ultimate in wedding entertainment. The wedding, from ceremony through the reception, would include actors and be scripted as part of a murder mystery. Professional event planners and a wedding party willing to learn their parts are a necessity to make this wedding one of the most unique. After all, how often does a wedding guest get to play detective and solve a murder?

The "Non-Wedding" Wedding Theme

This may be the ultimate surprise party that friends and family will ever attend. For couples who absolutely don't want to plan a major event, this could be their best option. To keep the lid on the surprise wedding, have the party at someone else's house. A "non-wedding" wedding can be held as a dinner party, informal pool party or picnic. For the ultimate party atmosphere, schedule the wedding for New Year's Eve or Halloween and come dressed as a bride and groom.

Certain formalities, such as a marriage license, will have to be obtained in advance. Arrange for a photographer, but have them hide the camera until the big news is revealed.

Picnic Theme

Everyone loves the sense of joy, family, playfulness and belonging that down home picnics embody. For a backyard wedding, set up picnic tables and benches around the backyard. Serve from a buffet and include a barbecue—the hallmark of all picnics.

Renaissance Theme

Bring out the white horses, knights and jesters. If the bride and groom have long fancied experiencing the age of chivalry and innocence, here's the perfect time and place to find that special prince or princess. This medieval, outdoor event is ideal for having guests come in costume. In keeping with the theme, send out fairy tale invitations. (see Invitations)

Large banners and family crests can herald the event, and woodwind, lute and harp players can provide the musical entertainment. Utensils are optional as everyone feasts on drumsticks. With some luck and lots of planning, this wedding theme might even be held at the site of a local Renaissance Faire.

Riverboat Gambler Theme

For couples who live near the Mississippi River, the wedding could take place on one of the old fashioned paddle boats that cruises the river. A banjo-playing Dixieland band and 1850s costumes would make for a riverboat blast.

Roaring Twenties Theme

Many tie the knot aboard cruise ships or ships like the Queen Mary—a noncommissioned ship that caters specially to tourists and weddings. For this theme, make the twenties come alive with dancing "flappers" and spirited big band music.

Safari or Sportsmen's Theme

This affair requires formal khakis with safari hats and bush jackets. And yes, zoos and wild animal parks really do accommodate weddings. With real honest-to-goodness wild game in the vicinity, imagine the great shots a photographer can get.

Sports Theme

When sports are the bride and groom's passion, they might want to consider having the wedding ceremony and reception at a golf club or tennis club. Even Bill Gates got married on the 17th hole of a golf course overlooking the ocean. So why not any bride and groom?

A sports club location might be the extent of the sports theme. However, the idea could be expanded upon to include, for example, golf or tennis designed centerpieces and cakes.

Theme Park Theme

There's nothing Mickey Mouse about a wedding that's complete with a crystal coach and Sleeping Beauty's Castle. That's because Disneyland and Disney World are ready to accommodate themes of every whim with reception halls to match.

Other theme parks, such as Knott's Berry Farm and Universal Studios Hollywood, also specialize in themed events and can make dreams come true. Universal has the special effects necessary to create almost any romantic location, including Victorian London, modern Paris and ancient Rome.

Victorian Theme

Numerous Victorian homes are available for weddings. Some are listed in the *National Register of Historical Places*. Some are actual museums, such as the *Kellogg Museum* in Southern California, which features a beautiful gazebo for the ceremony and shaded structure for the reception.

The bride and groom could hark back to the old days by having a Victorian porch ceremony while a musician plays a Victorian barrel organ. To find authentic clothes, ask family members about heirlooms, or search the classifieds and vintage clothing stores for that ivory lace dress or blouse. A high tea is the perfect catering companion to a Victorian wedding. As a crowning touch, have the baker prepare an original Victorian wedding fruitcake.

CHAPTER 23

TRANSPORTATION TURN-ONS

When Frank Sinatra sang the lyrics "Love and marriage, love and marriage, go together like a horse and carriage," he could have been referring to the way some couples embark on their new journey. A horse-drawn carriage is romantic, but there are other options just as unusual. Maybe more so.

Classic and Vintage Cars

- Classic or vintage automobiles may be just the element you're looking for. A mint condition classic car can whisk newlyweds from the wedding ceremony to the reception in style. Classic cars might even tie in to the theme. For example, one entire wedding party in California dressed up in Victorian clothes and drove a fleet of shiny Model T Fords to the reception.

- Want to get steamy right from the start? Set out in a vintage 1914 Stanley Steamer. The car roars like a jet plane about to take off, but the ride is as smooth as silk. It'll make for great pictures and great memories.

- Model T Fords provide a truly traditional look.

- Restored cars from the fifties, like the fin-tailed '57 Chevy or an early 1950s Cadillac, are definite crowd-pleasers.

- For the racier set, how about the classic '65 Ford Mustang or Corvette Convertible? Because the Corvette's a two-seater, drive it away without a chauffeur. But that shouldn't be a problem!

- Some people might want one of the late 60s and 70s "muscle cars," such as an Oldsmobile 442 or a 396 cubic inch engine Chevy Chevelle complete with mag wheels and rumbling headers.

- Want to get outrageous? For motorcycle enthusiasts, a Harley-Davidson Softail Custom motorcycle will whisk newlyweds away with a rumble. Or at least take the couple around the block where they can get into more appropriate wedding attire-style transportation. Besides, those helmets cause havoc to that hair you spent all that money on. Of course, only those who *absolutely* know how to ride a large motorcycle should attempt this.

How does one get a vintage or classic car? Inquire among friends and wedding guests. Find out if they know anyone who has a car that they'd be willing to part with for an afternoon. Contact vintage automobile clubs and find out if someone's willing to help out.

Certain car rental companies now rent classics such as Mustangs and other cars. Locate them in the local Yellow Pages. Start hunting around early and surely something exciting will get the newlyweds rolling in the right direction!

CHAPTER 24

VIDEOGRAPHY

Professional wedding videographers can add titles, special digital effects and fully edit the videotape. But for video that's more fun and unpredictable, here are two intriguing ideas.

Documentary

Yes, the bride and groom can star in their own documentary. Just find a future film director who will follow the couple around with a video camera as they shop for wedding gowns, look at invitations and go to the bridal shower. A mock proposal would make a perfect opening shot. To keep costs down, have the director try to edit in the camera.

Pass the Camcorder

The idea here is to have an amateur version of the wedding reception as videotaped by several guests. To make this idea work, obtain a camcorder that's easy to use. Next, a small number of friends can then be trained how to operate the camera. Then during the reception, each "trained" friend takes the camera for ten, fifteen, or twenty minutes before passing it along to the next amateur videographer.

It might be best to assign one knowledgeable person to help with any technical questions that might arise, such as white balancing or pausing, etc. The resulting video could be a lot of fun! Remember—this is NOT a substitute for a professional videographer.

CHAPTER 25

WEDDING ATTIRE

The many styles and fashions of gowns and accessories are much too numerous to mention. But here are a smattering of ideas that adopt a floral touch.

Floral Wreath Crown Headpiece

Lady Diana Spencer and singers Mariah Carey and Diana Ross wore tiara headpieces with sheer veils trailing from them. But for outdoor or garden weddings, a bride could do as Kathie Lee did when she wed Frank Gifford: She wore a beautiful floral wreath.

The floral wreath can be constructed with or without a veil. Although many floral wreaths are composed of roses, there's the Victorian style of orange blossoms. A circlet of flowers looks especially stunning on brides with long, flowing hair.

Flowers, Pearls and Ribbon Shoes

Cinderella, eat your heart out. No matter how ordinary the bridal shoes are, they can be transformed into dazzling slippers with a touch of the right miniature flowers, or pearls, and ever-so-dainty ribbon.

Get the glue gun ready and test out a design using an inexpensive pair of shoes—just to be sure that everything holds in place.

Floral Wedding Gown

Why not let nature lend a hand to make a wedding dress as pretty as a flower! Make a plain dress stunning and an elaborate dress spectacular with a dash of rose petals or miniatures around the hem of the gown, small clusters of flowers at the shoulder, and baby's breath sprinkled along the veil or headpiece. Use imagination to create floral bridesmaids' gowns as well.

Tuxedo Style

For brides who like the basic idea of "his and hers," there is the option of wearing a bridal tuxedo. This can be a formal black and white tux that matches the groom's. Or, it may include a custom blouse and decorative vest to set it apart from the groom's formal attire. A less formal tuxedo idea?—wear a very elegant all-white pants and jacket ensemble with a sheer or lace blouse.

Victorian Bridal Handbag

Brides and bridesmaids need not be dressed in Victorian attire to carry a dainty, satin Victorian handbag. To make each one personalized, these handbags can also decorated with silk flowers, imported French ribbons and a string of pearls.

The finished handbag is not only elegant, but is useful for those gift envelopes that may be handed to the bride.

Thai Silks— Though the name is Thai Silks, the company also carries cotton and silk linen blends from countries like Thailand, China, India, Japan and Korea. Imported fabrics, lingerie, scarves, and accessories are available. Thai Silks caters to both the retail and wholesale market. Tell them you heard about them in this book for a 10% discount. The catalog's free by calling 800-221-SILK.

Clothing & Sporting Goods

Campor— Good-bye city life! For hikers, backpackers and outdoor couples, this is a great catalog to distribute for bridal gifts. It's loaded with hundreds of useful sporting, camping and clothing items. Everything from tents, bikes, and roller blades to ski goods and backpacks are in the free catalog. Call 800-526-4784.

Eddie Bauer— Owned by Spiegel, Eddie Bauer offers high quality clothing and other merchandise. There's no bridal registry, but there are three different catalogs, including a Home Collection catalog. All catalogs are free. To order one or locate a store near you call 800-645-7467.

Lands' End Direct Merchants— Here's a premier mail order company known for standing behind its products. Lands' End combines both quality and value in comfortable, roomy clothing for men and women. In addition to clothing and clothing accessories, you'll find a line of snow boots, lightweight, rugged luggage sets and versatile, multi-pocketed attaches. For a free catalog, call 800-356-4444.

L.L. Bean, Inc.— Here's another place to look for sporting goods and clothing. Name most sports and they have the equipment, whether it's clothing, bicycles, skiing, boating, fishing, hunting, etc. L.L. Bean produces several catalogs yearly, including seasonal and special catalogs. For a free catalog, call 800-221-4221.

Fine Arts

The Art Institute of Chicago— This prestige museum has a store catalog that offers exquisite jewelry, books, prints, Christmas cards and other products. The catalog is produced in the fall. To obtain the free publication, call the store at 800-621-9337.

Barnes & Noble Bookstores, Inc.— While known as a huge book wholesaler, their large catalog includes books, CDs, audio tapes, and videotapes. But they also offer an art gift catalog. Filled with unique reproductions and gifts, it's called ART AND ARTIFACTS and comes out twice a year. For free catalogs, call 800-242-6657.

The Metropolitan Museum of Art— These gift shops offer reproductions of museum artwork, as well as sculpture, books, ceramics, jewelry and a cornucopia of other artistic delights. In addition to the New York store, satellite stores are located in California, Connecticut, Georgia, New Jersey, Ohio and Texas. While the main store in New York offers a bridal registry, the satellites don't yet have the service. For a free catalog and list of satellite locations, call 800-468-7386.

Museum of Fine Arts, Boston— This catalog offers paintings, sculpture, jewelry, clothing accessories, and other fine art items that represent masterpieces found in the museum. For a free catalog, call 800-225-5592.

The Museum of Modern Art— More modern than the Jetsons, the MOMA catalog delights with a see-through "teapot 2000," double helix flatware, decorator watches, telephones, furniture, pens and much, much more. It's fun to browse through the $3 catalog. To order the catalogs and products, call 800-447-MOMA.

Print's Graphic Design Book Store— Here's a book store dealing specifically with design topics and ideas. Send for a free catalog by calling 800-222-2654.

The Smithsonian Catalog— The Smithsonian Catalog offers some unique art gifts such as books, jewelry, scarves, ties, toys and other assorted items. While some of these products can be found elsewhere, many are exclusives that relate to the Smithsonian collection. For a free catalog call 800-322-0344.

Wireless— This catalog, produced by a not for profit organization whose proceeds are funneled into public radio and television, is filled with fun gifts of all sorts. Here's the place to find everything from classic videos and Garrison Keeler's *Prairie Home Companion Collection* to nostalgic memorabilia and a home brewing beer kit. There's also a catalog called *Signals*, which offers an upscale selection of products and videos. For a free catalog, call 800-669-9999.

Flowers, Gardening & Accessories

Jackson & Perkins— Here's where to find sundials, rose arches, cast iron planters and other backyard ornaments, as well as a host of other flower and garden items. They have a variety of catalogs that come out each season, including a *Christmas Catalog*. Order toll-free anytime of the day or night by calling 800-292-4769.

J.E. Miller Nurseries— J.E. Miller welcomes you to a wide world of horticulture, garden, and nursery supplies. The catalog is free. Call 800-836-9630.

Smith & Hawken— Seasonal and holiday catalogs include wreaths, plant gift sets, topiaries, teak furniture, backyard ornaments, books and even a professional flower press. For a free catalog, call 800-776-3336.

Home, Kitchen & Accessories

The Bombay Company— This company, with over 400 stores in the U.S. and Canada combined, features items for the home and kitchen that possess old world charm, class and elegance. Expect to find classical silver plate napkin rings, a brass-hinged memory album, a heart-shaped table and a jewelry wardrobe cabinet. For a free catalog, call a local Bombay Company store or 800-829-7789.

The Chile Shop— When looking for dinnerware that accentuates the American Southwest, The Chile Store, located in Santa Fe, New Mexico, offers a unique line of products. In addition to Mimbreño China based on that used in the historic Santa Fe Railroad dining car, there's a broad collection of stunning petroglyph pottery, etched glassware, crystal barware, stoneware, chile ornaments, and even gourmet gift baskets with spicy salsas, dips and treats. For information about the bridal registry and a catalog, call 505-983-6080

Colonial Garden Kitchens—Colonial Garden Kitchens
is a division of Hanover Direct (see Major Department Stores). Here's where you'll find small appliances and just about anything for use around the house. Their wares include items like cookware sets, baking dishes, pasta makers, tablecloths, microwave ovens, fondue pots, plant table stands and more. The catalog is free. Phone 800-752-5552.

Coming Home— A division of Land's End, Inc. this home collection catalog is where you'll find all kinds of bedding, linens, towels, curtains, wallpaper and more for the home. To make things easy for brides, the Coming Home catalog offers a bridal registry. Call for both the full Land's End catalog and Coming Home collection at 800-345-3696.

Crabtree & Evelyn— With over 175 stores in the United States and more around the world, Crabtree & Evelyn is a good bet for finding bridal shower gifts as well as teas and accessories for entertaining. They've got bath gels and lotions, colognes, toilet waters, towels, robes, slippers, mirrors, rugs, cobalt glass containers, floral wreaths and even garden hats. For entertaining you'll find comestibles like teas, cookies, biscuits, preserves, honeys and chutneys. Also available are a full line of tea accessories, including silver spoons, jam jars, tea infusers and strainers. Some products come prepackaged in attractive gift boxes or baskets. To obtain a free catalog or find a local store, call 800-253-1519.

Crate & Barrel— This popular retail chain has stylish furnishings and kitchenware for every room throughout the home. For added convenience they offer a bridal and gift registry, which can be contacted at 800-967-6696. The phone number for a free catalog is 800-323-5461.

Domestications— Another division of Hanover Direct, Domestications sells home accessories from comforters and bedding to waterbeds and tablecloths to candles and all sorts of decorative items. Domestications even has a collection that's available through Sears, Roebuck and Company. To get a free copy of this comprehensive home specialty catalog, just call 800-782-7722.

Lenox China & Crystal— High quality china for those who favor the more traditional designs and patterns. The catalog costs $2. Call 800-635-3669.

Reed & Barton— These highly renowned American silversmiths will set you up with sterling-plate, sterling silver and stainless flatware. For a free brochure, call them at 800-343-1383.

Williams-Sonoma— With over 100 stores nationwide, Williams-Sonoma has the goods to stock any kitchen from top to bottom. Their immense wonderland of kitchenware includes gadgets, appliances, cutlery, storage items and much more— not to mention over twenty different dinner china patterns. The company features a nationwide bridal registry. To take advantage of this convenient service, couples need to visit a store in order to register. For a free catalog and location of a local store, call 800-541-2233.

The Wooden Spoon— For stocking up the kitchen, look here for cookbooks, dishes, pans, utensils, cutting boards and more. From traditional cast iron skillets and cookware to the latest in electronic appliances, The Wooden Spoon catalog brims with shower and wedding gift ideas. For their free catalog call 800-431-2207.

Major Department Stores

Hanover Direct— Based in Hanover, Pennsylvania and in business for more than 50 years, this mail order firm is like several companies under one roof. They offer catalogs specializing in women's and men's fashions, home accessories, seniors and more. For the kitchen there's *Kitchen and Home* and *Colonial Garden Kitchens* catalog. There's also *Enchantments*, a new Christmas season catalog. All catalogs are free. Call 800-437-9686.

J.C. Penney Co., Inc.— J.C. Penney's bi-annual bridal catalog offers bridal gowns, bridesmaids' dresses and accessories. A Penney's Bridal Rep takes measurements over the phone, with gowns delivered within just 10 working days. Catalogs can be obtained at a Penney store. The bridal catalog is free. Call 800-222-6161.

Sears, Roebuck & Co.— Sears has discontinued their century-old mail order catalog and replaced it with Sears Shop At Home service, offered to people holding a Discover or Sears credit card. For more information call 800-366-3125.

Service Merchandise— The company refers to itself "America's Leading Jeweler." But they also carry products of every kind and for every taste. Best of all, Service Merchandise offers a convenient, computerized bridal registry system. Within five business days of completing their Gift Registry form, you'll get a computerized listing of your listed items. Guests can easily shop for gifts at over 370 stores nationwide or over the phone. For those who call, a Service Merchandise representative will explain all the items on the registry list. Gifts are sent out directly to the address the bride and groom request. Catalogs and bridal registry information forms are free by calling 800-251-1212.

Spiegel— Spiegel doesn't offer a bridal registry, but their extensive catalog carries most merchandise and gift items. Spiegel's sales catalogs are free, but their large catalogs cost $3 each. There is, however, a $3 certificate enclosed for a first purchase. You can also buy catalogs through some bookstores, such as Walden Books and B. Dalton. To order a catalog, call 800-345-4500.

Miscellaneous

Barbara Logan's Paperworks— These delicate, beautiful, distinctive and unique handmade papers make for really special bridal invitations. The varieties of papers range from natural and floral, to parfait and glitter. Invitations can be inked in almost any color. The company also offers printing. For free information and a sample of handmade paper, call 800-458-9143.

Basket of Fantasies— Known for their award-winning gift baskets, Basket of Fantasies customizes their ornately wrapped works of art with everything from gourmet food to elegant candles. Baskets come in all shapes, including heart-shaped, and can even be personalized by printing on the decorative ribbon. The company also offers a fun 21 piece Wedding Time Capsule kit that includes a "What Life Was Like" book that profiles the newlyweds and their parents, letters to the future stationery, time capsule seals and more. The company also delivers Bon Voyage gifts to cruise ships (So. California)—a great surprise for newlyweds, parents and visiting guests. For a free brochure, call them toll-free at 1-888-BASKET9. (1-888-227-5389)

Bernie's Discount Center— Brand name discounts on TVs, appliances, stereo and office equipment can be found at Bernie's, which has been in business for more than 40 years. For a $1 catalog, call 212-564-8758.

Brookstone— Brookstone's *Hard-To-Find-Tools* catalog contains a lot of items you wish you had but didn't know where to find, such as a coin counter, an aluminum can crusher, modular wine racks and home security products. Two seasonal catalogs, summer and Christmas, feature gift oriented items. For a free catalog call 800-926-7000.

The Celebration Fantastic— This is the catalog to open when you want everyday to be a holiday or celebration. Inside are lots of nifty gifts for both men and women. There are also several personalized wedding products: Private label wines, a wedding invitation music box, Christmas ornaments, ring boxes and even boxer shorts for the groom! Call for a free catalog at 800-527-6566.

Crutchfield Corporation— A Crutchfield catalog might provide audio and video buffs with the wedding gifts they want. There's home stereo and video equipment galore in the free catalog. Call 800-336-5566.

DAK— Crave the latest in microelectronics? The catalog is crammed with them. From LED tire gauges to multimedia computer upgrades, from bread makers to miniature TVs and CD changers. For a free catalog, call 800-DAK-0800.

Discount Bridal Service— Ever wish you had the inside track to a personalized buying service to help sort things out, handle the details, and get you the best prices? Then Discount Bridal Service, or DBS, may be just what you're looking for. This personalized buying service for brides can obtain many quality items and bridal accessories, from nationally advertised gowns and invitations, to headpieces and party favors, all discounted from retail prices. With its headquarters in Baltimore, the company has a network of over 400 helpful dealer representatives across the United States and Canada. Although DBS offers no catalog, they are a valuable bridal resource. Find the location of the nearest dealer by calling Discount Bridal Service at (800) 874-8794.

Exposures— Exposures offers a whole catalog of unique picture frames, albums, and other ways of storing photographic memories. For example, a favorite photo, such as one of the bride and groom, can be placed on a deck of playing cards. The company even offers an "heirloom book" kit which results in a professionally organized and custom-printed keepsake. For a catalog, call 800-222-4947.

Godiva Chocolatiers— Do you ever wake up in a chocolate sweat? If so, then you'll want to consider the three different mouth-watering wedding favors concocted by this well known Belgian chocolate maker. They come nestled in foil or gold boxes, decorated with flowers and the color-coordinated ribbon of your choice. They're ideal not only for weddings, but for rehearsals or showers. To get a glimpse of these rich chocolate memories, call Godiva at 800-643-1579.

Hammacher Schlemmer— This company is known for unusual, unconditionally guaranteed products that are rated among the best of their kind. You'll find everything from a Harley-Davidson Telephone to fax machines. They offer gift certificates. For a free catalog, call 800-233-4800.

Harry and David— Well known for their *Fruit-of-the-Month Club*, Harry and David provides many holiday and general purpose hand-packed gift baskets perfect for visiting guests or as bridal shower presents. Fruit, however, is just the beginning. Expect to find many luscious candies, cheesecakes, tortes, smoked turkeys, hams, and even decorative wreaths. For a free catalog call 800-547-3033.

Levenger— Looking for unusual gifts for members of the bridal party or for a home office bridal shower? Save time by perusing the Levenger catalog. It contains numerous nifty items, including day planners, fine pens, monogrammed "pocket briefcases," personalized business card cases, classic leather travel bags, book bags and even a contoured lap desk. Levenger also offers a wealth of intriguing, book-related items, such as lamps and ottomans. For a free catalog and helpful, responsive service, call 1-800-545-0242

New England Basket Co.— The company deals only with businesses. So have your florist, caterer, hotel banquet manager or wedding consultant call this basket and packaging distributor. With baskets shaped like hearts, Christmas sleighs, and of every shape, size, and color, your imagination will take flight. They've also got novelty containers, papier-mâché swans and decorative bird cages. In Massachusetts call 508-759-2000. Others call 800-524-4484.

Now & Forever— This catalog specializes in wedding invitations, many of them unique and personal. You'll also find unique wedding accessories and gifts for the entire bridal party—from the flower girls and bridesmaids to the groomsmen and best man. For a catalog, call 800-521-0584.

Personal Creations— If you want the personal touch of monograms on such things as picture frames and champagne glasses, Personal Creations can do the job. They'll provide the product; all you need is to provide the name. The free catalog is available by calling 800-326-6626.

Petrossian Paris— Petrossian Paris specializes in the delivery of the world's finest caviar, smoked salmon and foie gras right to your door via Federal Express. Their Russian caviar is highly reputed, as are all their products. Out-of-town guests will rave about this gourmet welcome gift. For a catalog, call 800-828-9241.

Private Cellars, Ltd.— This company can provide you with exquisitely decorated private label champagnes and wines. Private Cellars' selection of fine wines includes Cabernet Sauvignon, Chardonnay, Sauvignon Blanc and White Zinfandel. Bottle sizes range from individual favor and table sizes, to extra-large party-sized bottles. Gold-braided bottle necks and decorative hot wax seals will complement your private label message to make for memorable celebrations. For a free catalog, call Private Cellars, Ltd. at 800-800-4436.

The San Francisco Music Box Company— In business 15 years with 170 stores in 35 states, this company makes it easy to find enchanting music boxes. They even have musical cake toppers. One features a dancing couple beneath a lantern-lit gazebo. Yet another popular model features doves on a book of love while playing *The Wind Beneath My Wings*. The color catalog is free and includes a $5 coupon for use towards a purchase. Call 800-227-2190.

The Sharper Image— Known for carrying really nifty electronic gadgets, The Sharper Image has expanded into high quality items of all sorts, including clothing, luggage and stereo equipment. The full-size juke boxes, scale model cars and movie sculptures will capture your fancy. They offer gift certificates. For a free catalog or the location of a store in your neighborhood, call 800-344-4444.

Starbucks Coffee Company— With over 3,000 stores and growing, Starbucks offers a catalog full of coffee and coffee-related gift items. How about the gift of coffee beans delivered fresh to a bride and groom's home? There's all the appliances for making a great cup of coffee, including mugs, candies, cookies, coffee cake, jams, and just about everything needed to start the morning off right. A special holiday catalog includes gift baskets with baskets for all budgets. For a free catalog, call 800-782-7282.

The Timeless Touch— This Georgia-based company preserves your flowers for you after the wedding. They send you a special temperature-controlled shipping box, which you return to them packed with your flowers. When they're done, you'll get your flowers arranged three-dimensionally in a variety of attractive shadow box presentations. For a brochure call 800-688-6085.

Victoria's Secret— Less is definitely more when it comes to this well known lingerie store. To find the shop nearest you, call 800-HER-GIFT. Ordering by phone is available 24 hours a day. To receive a free catalog, call 800-477-9977.

Waldenbooks— Books for all tastes, including bridal showers, are found here. From how-to books for bettering home and garden to humor and everything in between. Any book can be ordered, even if it's not in the catalog. Call 800-322-2000.

Webway, Inc.— At last, a company with a variety of high quality, affordable wedding photo albums. Webway offers attractive bonded leather albums and archival mat pages for much less than most photographers charge for equivalent products. Of course, you'll probably have to organize your own wedding album photos. For a free catalog and the address and number of the closest retailer, call 800-328-2344.

The Wine Enthusiast— This catalog offers unique gifts including wine-related apparel—such as silk ties, t-shirts and cuff links—not to mention the most advanced corkscrews, gift bottle wrappings, wine cellars, glasses, wine luggage, and even customized plaques that can be personalized as a special gift. To get information about *The Wine Enthusiast's* bridal registry or to get a free catalog, call 800-356-8466.

The Woodworkers' Store— For tools, wood, hardware and information on building handmade gifts from large to small, this is an excellent resource. With stores nationwide and an extensive catalog, expect to find items such as precision tools, turned pen sets, clock kits, and even a collection of historical paint colors. For a free catalog, call 800-279-4441.

Index

R

rafting party 5
receptions 87-91
recipe shower 21
registries (see bridal)
renaissance theme 102
riverboat theme 103
roaring '20s theme 103
roasting party 6

S

sachet; potpourri favor 78
safari theme 103
Santa Claus 70
seashell centerpiece 39
shoes 110
silhouette invitation 62
sites 65-66
skiing party 6
sports party 7
sports theme 103
square dance caller 71
stationery holder favor 78
steel drum band 70
stenciled invitation 62
sterling picture frame 78
storybook characters 50
sushi bar 33

T

table settings 95-98
    cake look-alike 95
    holiday garlands 95
    lobster bibs 97
napkin holders 96 -98
    pictures 97
    skirt decorations 98
tea 9, 21, 32-33
theatrical rental 42
theme parks 7, 103
themes 99-104
time capsule shower 22
time of day shower 22
tiramisu cake 29
topiary centerpiece 39
transportation 105-106
treasure candle 40

U

unity candle 44

V

Valentine's Day 40
Victorian
    bridal handbag 87, 110
    fan 15
    fan cake 29
    invitations 53
    napkin rings 98
    photography 81
    porch ceremony 104
    wedding fruitcake 104
    wedding theme 104
videography 69, 107
    documentary 107
Viennese coffee bar 10, 31
vintage automobiles 105-106
volleyball party 7

W

water and juice bar 10
waterpark party 7
wedding attire
    bridal handbag 110
    floral headpiece 109
    floral gown 110
    tuxedo style 110
    wedding cake favor 78
wedding consultants 1
wedding favors 73-79
wedding locations 65-66
wedding plaque 91
wedding quilt shower 22
wedding sites 104
Wedgwood cake 29
welcome baskets 79, 111, 121
white bar 11
white wedding desserts 47
wine & cheese party 8
wine lover's shower 23
wok station 33
wreath centerpiece 40

PLANNING & CREATIVE IDEAS

Use the following pages to list favorite ideas or even to plan your wedding... memorably, of course!

Wedding Sites and Ceremony—
CREATIVE IDEAS:

FACTS & PHONE NUMBERS:

BUDGET & PRICE QUOTES:

Gowns and Tuxes—
CREATIVE IDEAS:

FACTS & PHONE NUMBERS:

BUDGET & PRICE QUOTES:

Bouquets, Flowers and Centerpieces—
CREATIVE IDEAS:

FACTS & PHONE NUMBERS:

BUDGET & PRICE QUOTES:

Catering, Cake and Favors—
CREATIVE IDEAS:

FACTS & PHONE NUMBERS:

BUDGET & PRICE QUOTES:

Photography & Videography—
CREATIVE IDEAS:

FACTS & PHONE NUMBERS:

BUDGET & PRICE QUOTES:

Entertainment and Invitations—
CREATIVE IDEAS:

FACTS & PHONE NUMBERS:

BUDGET & PRICE QUOTES:

DO YOU WANT A DREAM WEDDING,
BUT THINK YOU CAN'T AFFORD ONE?

The *Dream Wedding Video* helps brides and grooms make their most special day come true...*easily and affordably*:

- √√ SAVE 20-40% on nationally advertised gowns
- √√ SAVE 50% on a musical ensemble
- √√ SAVE 50% or more on a wedding cake
- √√ SAVE $100 or more on a photo album alone
- √√ FIND the best services and not get ripped off
- √√ SAVE time of having to dig thru wedding guides
- √√ ENTERTAIN the whole family with 1-hr. fun video
- √√ PLUS many more money saving secrets

"Budget conscious wedding planners will welcome this excellent program" **Booklist Magazine**

"A cornucopia of money saving tidbits...a pennywise guide to shaving a grand here and there off the wedding bill. And the tips are excellent." **R. Pittman, Video Reviewer**

There's never been an easier way to stretch your wedding dollars beyond what you thought possible. The video is like having a personal advisor who gives you the benefit of their wealth of knowledge, expertise, strategies and secrets. Order from this coupon and SAVE $5.00 off the $24.95 price.

CLIP OUT THIS COUPON FOR QUICK ORDERING

Qty ___ **Dream Wedding *Video* @ $19.95 each** _____

Shipping & Handling $5.00 per each unit: _____

Californians **ONLY** add $1.65 tax per unit: _____

                         TOTAL: _____

Name_____

Street Address_____

City, State, Zip_____

Send Check/   **MOON LAKE MEDIA**
Money Order To: **"DREAM WEDDING VIDEO"**
                    P.O. BOX 251466
             LOS ANGELES, CA 90025

Allow 2-4 Weeks for Delivery